HEROIC YEARS

HEROIC YEARS

Louisiana in the War for Southern Independence

WBRZ-TV
1964
Lectures in Louisiana
History

By

EDWIN ADAMS DAVIS

Bureau of Educational Materials and Research
College of Education
Louisiana State University
Baton Rouge, Louisiana

Printed by Vail-Ballou Press, Inc., Binghamton, N.Y.

FOR

Eddie and Mary Claire

IN MEMORIAM

". . . I have been true to my promises (reading my bible). . . . I have been a faithful soldier to my country, never shunning duty, but always ready to go when it came my time."

—Jack P. Myers
Third Louisiana Infantry

(From a letter to his mother, original in possession of Mrs. Joseph E. Zimmer, Bloomfield, Connecticut. Copy through the courtesy of Margaret Lee, Monroe, Louisiana.)

Foreword

The ability to chronicle events of a hundred years ago, so as to bring these bygone events alive in today's stream of life is a rare talent. Yet, this feat has been accomplished in this volume by Edwin Adams Davis with great skill and feeling. Many thousands of pages have been written about "The War Between the States," but none of these writings has been presented in a more engaging style than that of Dr. Davis in his "Heroic Years."

Perhaps this is due to the fact that "Heroic Years" is really a television series, prepared at the specific request of WBRZ-TV. Late in 1960 and early in 1961 Dr. Davis appeared on the station with two programs that told of the start of the Civil War when Louisiana seceded from the Union and rushed into the emotional war years ahead. The audience reaction to these programs prompted us to ask Dr. Davis to conduct a study of the fascinating history of the war as it was in all of the state. We requested that the series be designed for "general public" acceptance, and especially for students of Louisiana history. The result is "Heroic Years," a most entertaining television series and a romantic and informative narrative of the most fateful period in the development of Louisiana.

WBRZ-TV is, therefore, deeply grateful to Dr. Davis, and to the Bureau of Educational Materials and Research of Louisiana State University for its co-operation in the publication of the television manuscript.

Douglas L. Manship
President and General Manager
WBRZ-TV

Preface

Louisiana seceded from the United States on January 26, 1861, and two months later joined the newly organized Confederate States of America. United States President Abraham Lincoln refused to recognize the right of a state to secede and the legality of the new Southern republic. On April 15 he declared that "insurrection" existed and called for 75,000 volunteers to suppress "combinations" in the South "too powerful to be suppressed by the ordinary course of judicial proceedings." The war to force the seceded states back into the American Union soon began.

The following four years, from 1861 to 1865, were the heroic years of Louisiana—youthful enthusiasms of new nationality, patriotic mobilizing of strength for its defense, the valiant patriotism of her soldiers, the sufferings of her people from the hardships of war and from armed invasions, the gradual wearing out of men and matériel, the final agony of defeat.

The war between the United States of America and the Confederate States of America has been called by many names. It was officially titled "The War of the Rebellion" until 1950 when Public Law 834 recognized the title which generally has been used in the South —"The War Between the States." In the interest of brevity most Southerners have called it simply "The War," while modern writers and historians have referred to it as "The Civil War," despite the fact that for four years the Confederate States of America was a living republic with its own government, armies, navy, and with a flag known throughout the world. Other names have included: "The Brothers War," "The War for the Union," and "The American Iliad." About thirty-five years ago New England historian Edward Channing titled it "The War for Southern Independence," and this name, in this writer's opinion, is the most accurate.

In terms of the size of armies, number of casualties, total military enlistments and civilian participants, intensity of fighting, size and varying character of terrain, utilization of economic resources, military and naval innovations, this war was the greatest the world had known. The boldness and individual genius of both Northern and Southern military leaders, coupled with the industrial and technological revolution of that era, brought innumerable innovations in weapons, matériel, transportation, and tactics, as well as in organization, logistics, and strategy.

The war was a struggle between the total economic resources, transportation facilities, manpower, and industrial production of the two nations, and in every category of comparison the North held from double to many times the advantage over the South. The great mystery of the war was why it took the North so long to force the surrender of the Confederate armies, armies which for months and months had been unable to secure adequate replacements and the fundamental necessities with which a soldier wages battle.

Among the noted civil and military leaders Louisiana furnished the Confederacy are included: Cabinet Member Judah P. Benjamin; Diplomats John Slidell, Pierre Rost, and A. B. Roman; Congressmen Charles M. Conrad, Duncan F. Kenner, Henry Marshall, Lucius J. Dupre, Thomas J. Semmes, Edward Sparrow, John Perkins, Jr., and Charles J. Villere; and Generals P. G. T. Beauregard, Richard Taylor, Braxton Bragg, Leonidas Polk (Episcopal Bishop of Louisiana who was called "The Fighting Bishop"), Paul O. Herbert, St. John R. Liddell, Alfred Mouton, Francis T. Nicholls, Leroy A. Stafford, Henry Watkins Allen, and Albert G. Blanchard.

Louisiana's soldiers left their blood, and many found shallow graves, in the far-off valleys of Virginia, Tennessee, Georgia, and other Southern states, as well as in their native state—at Baton Rouge, Labadieville, Port Hudson, Grand Coteau, Mansfield, Pleasant Hill, and at 600 lesser-known, but hard-fought engagements. Nearly 25 per cent of Louisiana's nearly 60,000 soldiers were killed in battle, died of wounds, or succumbed to various diseases during the war years. Of 135 men from Bastrop, for example, only 35 returned after the war ended. The Fourth, Thirteenth, and Nineteenth Louisiana regiments lost approximately one third of their commands at the Battle of Shiloh.

No man or woman lives who remembers those heroic years from 1861 to 1865. We of the South and of Louisiana are the grandchildren and great grandchildren of the men and women who made those years heroic, who were finally defeated in a long and bloody war, who gave of themselves and of all they possessed for an independent Southern Confederacy which became a "Lost Cause."

To their descendants these men and women bequeathed a heritage of formality and courtesy and personal honor, and a strong and possesive affection for home and parish, state and the Confederacy, and for the reunited nation, for they appreciated, more perhaps than have any other Americans because of having lived through four years of war and twelve years of military occupation, that a man has but one birthplace and one country and that these may be the most important factors in his life.

And few of them realized that because of their courage and fortitude during those sixteen holocaustic years they had added an inspiring tower to the great citadel of history.

No author can ever hope to make a complete acknowledgment of all the assistance and all the courtesies he has received in the course of his work; he can only name the persons to whom he feels most indebted. This author, therefore, is under obligation to many persons, including: Charles C. Phillips, Feature Editor of the Shreveport *Journal;* Mrs. Virginia Robicheaux, Librarian of the Shreveport *Times;* Professor W. Darrell Overdyke, Centenary College, Shreveport; Raymond H. Downs, Acting Director, State Archives and Records Commission; Mrs. Lena Y. deGrummond of the State Department of Education; Dr. E. B. Robert, Dean Emeritus of the College of Education, Louisiana State University; Wade O. Martin, Jr., Secretary of State of Louisiana; Dean Lemos L. Fulmer of the College of Education, Louisiana State University; Professor J. R. Brown, Northeast Louisiana State College, Monroe; C. C. Stephens, United Gas Corporation, Shreveport; Dr. Jo Ann Carrigan, Managing Editor, and Mrs. Elizabeth L. Lane, Secretary, *Louisiana History;* Mrs. Jacqueline Vidrine, Ville Platte, Louisiana; Ezra Adams, State Department of Agriculture; Theodore N. McMullan, Director, Louisiana State University Library; V. L. Bedsole, Head, Mrs. Virginia M. Ott, Registrar of Manuscripts, and Marcelle F. Schertz, Reference Archivist, Department of Archives, Louisiana State University Library; Evangeline Lynch, Louisiana Room, Edith Simms, Government Documents, and Helen H. Palmer, Humanities Division, Louisiana State University Library; Professor A. Otis Hebert, Jr., Francis T. Nicholls State College, Thibodaux, former Managing Editor of *Louisiana History;* Alva and Ed Sweeny, Aled's Resort, False River, Ventress, Louisiana; Max and Margaret Bradbury, Shreveport; John Laurent, Superintendent, Engraving Department, Baton Rouge *State-Times.*

Special acknowledgment must be given to Douglas L. Manship, President and General Manager, and John Ferguson, Program Manager, WBRZ-TV, who conceived and developed the original general plan of these lectures as a station series presentation; to Dr. John L. Loos, Chairman of the Department of History, Louisiana State University, for numerous favors both personal and professional; to Dr. Burl Noggle, Department of History, Louisiana State University, for judicious and critical assistance of high quality; to Donald Ellegood, former Director of the Louisiana State University Press, who contributed so much to the general organization and content of the lectures and who hoped to publish them; to Mrs. Mary L. McMinn, Charleston, West Virginia, critic and editor of the entire manuscript, who saved the writer from numerous errors of commission and omission; to Assistant Dean Donald E. Shipp of the College of Education and former Director of the Bureau of Educational Materials and Research, Louisiana State University, Dr. J. Berton

Gremillion, Director of the Bureau, and Mrs. Jeanette Hebert, Editorial Assistant and Secretary, who planned and executed the publication of the lectures; to John Crowe, Production Manager, and Mrs. Harry Evans, Special Projects, WBRZ-TV, who directed and produced the television lectures; to Martin J. S. Broussard, for special personal assistance during the preparation of the lectures; to Hazel L. Taylor, Secretary of the Department of History, Louisiana State University, who typed the lectures and the television outlines; to Doctor R. C. Kemp, for invaluable special personal assistance during the preparation and presentation of these lectures; to Michael Sotille, Head of the Photoduplications Department, Louisiana State University Library, who was responsible for all of the photographic illustrative material used in the lectures; to Dr. John A. Hunter, President of Louisiana State University, who helped plan the organization and content of the lectures nearly four years before they were presented; and to the author's wife, La Verna Rowe Davis, for having been an active collaborator, as she has always been, during all stages of the research for and writing of these lectures.

Edwin Adams Davis

Baton Rouge, 1964

Contents

I

Gathering Clouds—The Long Road to Secession

The Sectional Controversy. "Two opposing civilizations are in conflict here, and have been from the infancy of our Union." Thus wrote Andover (Massachusetts) Theological Seminary Professor Austin Philips concerning the sectional controversy which had developed between the North and the South during the years prior to 1860. Northern novelist Nathaniel Hawthorne phrased his opinion only slightly differently: "We never were one people, and never really had a country since the Constitution was formed." Numerous other Northern intellectual, religious, and political leaders agreed with Philips and Hawthorne.

In the South, proslavery protagonist Senator James H. Hammond of South Carolina emphatically argued that "no two nations on earth are, or ever were, more distinctly separated and hostile than we are. Not Carthage and Rome, England and France at any period." The Charleston *Mercury* reiterated the same sentiments: "The North and South are two nations, made by their institutions, customs and habits of thought, as distinct as the English and French; and our annual meetings at Washington are not congresses to discuss the common interests, but conventions, to contest antagonistic opinions and to proclaim mutual grievances and utter hostile threats." Numerous Southerners from Maryland to Texas agreed with Senator Hammond and the *Mercury*.

With such opinions emanating from the intelligent leadership of the North and of the South during the late years of the ante bellum period, it should not have been surprising that ideas of separation from the Union and of a Southern nationality at last reached maturity, that the Southern states seceded, and that they organized the Confederate States of America. As well-known historian Avery Craven has written: " . . . coexistence was rendered difficult if not impossible by the assumption on the part of each section that it represented the true American expression as envisaged by the founding fathers and embodied in the Constitution. Neither thought of itself as struggling for something new. Each was defending the

1

old. Each was innocent of wrong; each was confident of virtue."

After three quarters of a century in the old Union, the South took a strongly fixed position in defense of the sovereignty of the states, self-determination of civil rights, and the protection of Southern institutions and way of life; the North took an equally strong stand on national governmental authority rather than state rights, bitterly attacked the institution of slavery, and loudly proclaimed the self-righteous belief that there was a moral law higher than the Federal Constitution.

The issues, problems, subjects, principles of government, and practical economic and political questions over which the two sections differed were numerous, but the most important of them included internal improvements, additions of territory, tariffs, money and banking, foreign and domestic commerce, admission of new states, foreign relations, location of transcontinental railroads, constitutional powers of the states in relation to the powers of the Federal government, public-land policies, and the institution of slavery—the most important of all.

It is certain that had there been no Negroes in the United States, there would have been no institution of slavery, and had there been no institution of Negro slavery, the other issues of the North-South controversy most likely would have been compromised. The slave Negro, then, and the political, economic, social, and moral questions relative to his enslavement were the issues over which there could be no compromise. Slavery was the one factor which keynoted the South's intense, highly emotional belief in, and defense of, the principle of state rights; and it, therefore, was the indirect cause of secession. The election of the Republican party's Abraham Lincoln as President was the immediate cause of secession, and the war which followed was the result of the Federal government's decision that the Southern states had no constitutional right to secede from the United States and organize a new nation, and that they must be forced back into the old Union.

The Institution of Slavery. In view of the fact that slavery was of paramount importance in the South's position on the rights of states to determine their own institutions, it is necessary to survey briefly the origin and development of that particular institution.

In 1619 the first Negroes were brought to Virginia, where they, just as many whites, were sold for varying periods of time as indented servants. Within a few years enterprising Dutch and English shipmasters began to sell colored servants in all of the Atlantic seaboard colonies. Massachusetts legalized slavery in 1641, and Connecticut passed a similar law nine years later. During the 1660's New York, New Jersey, Maryland, and Virginia legalized the institution, and by the century's end it had been accepted in all the colonies.

Comparatively few Negroes were imported during the 1600's, however, and by 1700 they totaled only 5 per cent of the population.

2

But by 1775 approximately 20 per cent of all American colonials were Negro slaves, three fourths of whom were owned in the Southern colonies.

Slave labor was used chiefly in agriculture, and the small-scale, diversified agricultural system of the North could not use slave labor as profitably as could the large-scale, staple-crop agricultural system of the South. Northern manufacturers and businessmen also came to the conclusion that free, wage labor was cheaper than slave labor. It was not long before many slave masters of New England and Middle Atlantic colonies began to free their slaves and then to rehire them at low wages as free labor. The market for Negro slaves in the North, therefore, declined, and ship captains soon discovered that they could sell African slaves at much higher prices in the South.

During the period prior to the Revolution many colonial leaders, including such Southerners as Henry Laurens and Thomas Jefferson, seriously questioned the moral, religious, humanitarian, and economic aspects of the institution of slavery. The invention of the cotton gin, the discovery of the sugar-granulation process, and the increase in the world market for cotton, tobacco, and sugar, however, fixed the hold of large-scale, staple-crop agriculture and Negro slavery on the South.

The Years of Protest and Compromise, 1785–1830. Northern states began to abolish the institution of slavery just before the Revolution and by 1804 all of them had provided for the gradual emancipation of all slaves. But the institution continued in the North for many years, for Negroes were held in bondage in New York until 1827 and a few in scattered areas until 1846. In no Northern state were the Free Negroes permitted to assume the responsibilities of citizenship nor were they even granted the basic constitutional rights of free men.

Organized, nationwide agitation against slavery began with the founding of the New York City Manumission Society in 1785 and the Pennsylvania Abolition Society in Philadelphia four years later. Active leaders in these organizations included such national figures as John Jay, Alexander Hamilton, and Benjamin Franklin.

Thomas Jefferson proposed as early as 1776 to send the Negroes back to Africa, and the American Colonization Society was eventually established in 1817. Henry Clay, John Randolph, James Monroe, Bushrod Washington, James Madison, John Marshall, and other prominent Southerners were leaders in the organization, which by 1826 had a total of 143 local societies, 103 of them in the South. The Republic of Liberia was the outgrowth of the colonization plan, and Monrovia, the capital, was settled in 1822. Several Louisianians played active roles in the colonization movement.

Throughout these years the issue of slavery plagued the political leaders of the nation. During the Constitutional Convention of 1787 there was considerable debate on slavery, which resulted in various

3

slavery compromises. The issue was a factor in the location of the national capital at Washington and the establishment of the Federal District. It led to the Missouri Compromise of 1820, about which John Quincy Adams wrote: "I take it for granted that the present question is a mere preamble—a title-page to a great, tragic volume." But throughout these years the leaders of the North and South were able to compromise their differences regarding the institution without too much difficulty, for minds, not emotions, generally governed the thoughts and actions of men. The day was not far off when this would no longer be true.

..*The Abolitionist Attack upon the South, 1831–50.* The year 1831 was a fateful one in the controversy between North and South. On January 1, Northern antislavery crusader William Lloyd Garrison began the publication of the *Liberator,* a militant journal dedicated to the immediate abolition of slavery. Garrison proclaimed that the Constitution was "a convenant with death and an agreement with hell," that he favored "unconditional emancipation," that he would not retreat "a single inch," and that "I will be heard." The North, as represented by the Abolitionists, had become the self-appointed guardian of Southern morality and the Southern conscience.

In August, 1831, in Southampton County, Virginia, Negro preacher Nat Turner led a slave revolt during which over fifty people, mostly women and children, were murdered. Although Turner and the other leaders were soon captured, given a regular judicial trial, convicted, and hanged, a shock of horror swept through the South; for it was generally believed that the Abolitionists had indirectly, if not directly, encouraged the insurrection.

During the following winter a Virginia Convention, after exhaustive debates covering the whole slavery question, rejected all proposals for the emancipation of slaves in that state. This was the last Southern attempt to abolish the institution, and soon the Southern states began to tighten their regulatory slave laws.

The abolitionist attack rapidly gained momentum. The American Antislavery Society was founded in 1833 and by 1840 had over 2,000 local organizations. Oberlin College in Ohio became a center of western abolitionism. The Underground Railroad provided secret stations through which escaped slaves were transported to Canada. The Liberty party was founded in 1840 and the Free Soil party eight years later to attack "the aggressions of the slave power."

With vehement hearts rather than with rational minds, the Abolitionists pictured the South as they firmly believed it to be—"backward, tumbledown, ignorant, and immoral." They painted crude caricatures of both the slave and the slaveholder, although not acquainted with either; the slave was an angel of earth while his master was a whip-bearing, devil-incarnate villain. Southerners soon came to believe that it was necessary for Abolitionists to have something to persecute and that, having burnt all their witches, they had invented abolitionism in order to have a resource for new persecutions.

As the years passed from 1835 to 1861 the writings of the abolitionist group increased in intensity. They damned the South and all things Southern in language uniquely foul in American history. Never before, nor since, have the public men of one section so attacked their fellow Americans who were citizens of another section. One Louisiana editor wrote that they "abused and vilified us, exhausting the vocabulary of Billingsgate for epithets foul enough to designate us, proclaiming them from their . . . newspapers, and their pulpits. . . . [We] are held up to the gaze of an eager world as slave-drivers, lost to humanity and accursed of God, driving the slave around the cotton field with thongs red in his own gore, like the veriest beasts of burden, when at last too old to be driven more, and useless, we are represented as, with cold-blooded and devilish barbarity, knocking out his brains."

In 1849, for example, novelist Herman Melville in his fictional *Mardi* damned irrevocably the wicked slaveholder: "Let that master thrice shrive his soul; take every sacrament; on his bended knees give up the ghost; yet shall he die despairing; and live again, to die forever damned." Six years later William Lloyd Garrison wrote that the Southerner's "career from the cradle to the grave is but one of unbridled lust, of filthy amalgamation, of swaggering braggadocio, of haughty domination, of cowardly ruffianism, of boundless dissipation, of matchless insolence, of infinite self-conceit, of unequalled oppression, of more than savage cruelty." Even as late as April, 1865, after the surrender of Generals Robert E. Lee and Joseph E. Johnston, Minister Henry Ward Beecher wrote that no timber grown in the South's "cursed soil is fit for the ribs of our ship of state or for our household homes," that the Southerner's "honor is not honor, but a bastard quality . . . and for all times the honor of the supporters of slavery will be throughout the world a byword and a hissing."

Southerners sprang to the defense of the South, Southern institutions, and the Southern way of life. While they were never quite able to match the vitriolic diatribes of Northern fanatics, they frequently defended themselves graphicly. Minister James H. Thornwell of South Carolina, for example, wrote that the struggle was between "atheists, socialists, communists, red republicans, Jacobins on the one side, and the friends of order and regulated freedom on the other."

The final thunderous rumblings which portended the eruption of the American volcano were about to begin.

The Fateful 1850's. It was generally believed that the Compromise of 1850 would settle "with finality" the major problems of the two feuding sections. Daniel Webster in his seventh of March speech had spoken, not "as a Northern man, but as an American," and the New Orleans *Daily Crescent* shouted: "The phantom of

5

disunion is retiring before an awakened, healthful public interest. . . . The sentiment of *'liberty and union, one and inseparable,'* is at length thoroughly aroused in the capital of the nation." But the dissension did not die. Each year of the decade was to bring incidents to keep the controversy at fever pitch and even to fan the flames of its ever reddening fires.

In 1851 tension was increased by the Southern support, particularly in Louisiana, of the Lopez Cuban revolt against Spain, to which the North was strongly opposed.

On March 20 of the following year Harriet Beecher Stowe, sister of noted Abolitionist Henry Ward Beecher, published *Uncle Tom's Cabin,* a maudlin and sentimental novel purporting to be an accurate and true picture of the brutality and injustice of slavery. Mrs. Stowe's total acquaintance with the South consisted of one short visit to a Kentucky plantation and perhaps a few picnicking excursions across from Cincinnati to the southern shores of the Ohio River, and she later admitted that she knew nothing of the institution of slavery. The Mobile *Advertiser* soberly and rather accurately stated that the book was a concoction of "absurdities, falsehoods and inconsistencies," but the New Orleans *Crescent* emphasized that Mrs. Stowe was "part quack and part cut-throat," coming as a physician with arsenic in one hand and a pistol in the other, to treat diseases she had "never witnessed," and that "without having ever in her life beheld even a mouse," she had suddenly become "a great rat-catcher," modestly insisting "upon burning down our houses in order to rid us of a rat."

The first 5,000-copy edition of *Uncle Tom's Cabin* was sold in two days, 20,000 copies the first three weeks, over 300,000 copies by the end of the year, and over 1,250,000 copies the first eighteen months. It was soon translated into a dozen languages and in 1853 was written as a play. The book and the play inflamed the people of both North and South, and the teen-age Northern lads of the 1850's who read and believed in the accuracy of the book were the men who in 1860 elected Lincoln President.

The Republican party was organized in 1854 to combat slavery and its extension in the Federal Territories. In 1855 and 1856 proslavery and antislavery settlers struggled for the political control of Kansas. In May, 1856, a proslavery party raided and sacked Lawrence; a short time later fanatical John Brown, with seven companions including his four sons, massacred five Southerners at Henry's Crossing on Pottawatomie Creek. Guerrilla warfare began to rage throughout Kansas Territory.

Democrat James Buchanan was elected President in the fall of 1856, and many political leaders believed that things would now quiet down. But two days after Buchanan's inauguration the Supreme Court handed down its decision in the case of Negro Dred Scott, who had sued for freedom from slavery on the grounds that he had lived for some years with his master in Northern free territory. The court decided against Scott, and the decision was hailed as a great victory for the South. The following year Stephen A. Douglas and Abraham Lincoln campaigned for a senatorship in Illinois, attracting national attention because the beliefs of the two candidates were rather completely aired in a series of public debates. Lincoln rejected the theory of Negro equality but insisted that slavery was "a moral, a social, and a political wrong," and emerged from the debates as the great champion of the antislavery forces. He lost this election, but gained reputation enough to become the Republican candidate for President two years later.

At the beginning of 1859 the nation was quiet, but tense. A few months earlier, however, Lincoln's "House Divided" speech had asserted that "a house divided against itself cannot stand. I believe this government cannot endure permanently half slave and half free. I do not expect the Union to be dissolved; I do not expect the house to fall; but I do expect it will cease to be divided. It will become all one thing, or all the other," and New York Senator William H. Seward had reiterated that an "irrepressible conflict" existed between the North and South and that the country must sooner or later become a slaveholding nation or a free-labor nation.

The South, which had known some successes in its struggle with the North, now began to remember only the rebuffs and repulses, the frustrations and failures. *Uncle Tom's Cabin* had become "The Iliad of the Blacks." Henry Ward Beecher had said that in the struggle for Kansas a Sharpe's rifle was a greater moral agency than the Bible. William H. Seward had argued for a "Higher Law" than the Constitution for nearly a decade. Reason and logic fled the minds of the political leaders of both North and South. Only a spark was needed to inflame an entire nation; that spark was ignited on October 16, 1859.

Following his bloody Kansas raid in May, 1856, John Brown had moved eastward with a plan for inciting a slave insurrection in Virginia. The plan was made known to several prominent men in the North, some of whom contributed money for its execution. Brown assumed the name of Smith and rented a farm in Maryland, a few miles from Harpers Ferry, Virginia. On Sunday night, October 16, 1859, he led a party of eighteen men, including three of his sons, across the Potomac. He occupied the Harpers Ferry United States Armory, arsenal and rifle works, in the process killing the town's mayor and four other persons. After securing hostages, he sent word throughout the neighboring countryside that the slaves would soon be freed, but two days later he was captured and his expedition broken up by Colonel Robert E. Lee, who had been sent from Washington, D.C., with eighty marines.

Brown was indicted by a grand jury, tried before the Circuit Court of Jefferson County at Charlestown, and convicted on charges of rebellion against Virginia, inciting a slave insurrection, and murder. He was hanged on December 2.

7

Brown immediately became a martyr to the abolitionist cause. Ralph Waldo Emerson wrote that he had made "the gallows as glorious as the Cross." Henry David Thoreau, at a Concord (Massachusetts) church meeting, said: "Some eighteen hundred years ago Christ was crucified; this morning, perchance, Captain Brown was hanged. . . . He is not Old Brown any longer; he is an angel of light." To the people of the South, Brown was an angel of destruction and insurrection and death. He had led an armed invasion of the South to start an armed uprising of slaves to massacre whites—and the North had supported and applauded the action.

December, 1859. As the last days of 1859 passed, the people of Louisiana and of the entire South realized that concerning the antislavery movement and the abolitionist crusade against the South, they were now facing fact, not theory; they were now facing direct action involving physical force, not the speeches of agitators. The fanatics of the North had supported John Brown; they would support other such actions in the future.

As Southerners looked back over the years of the American nation and the attacks to which they had been subjected, many of them began to seriously evaluate the worth of the Union. Fire-eating extremists urged immediate secession; middle-of-the-roaders and conservatives pleaded for time to calm the impetuous ones and to work out compromises to the problems plaguing the Union.

Louisiana's gubernatorial election was held on November 7, 1859, three weeks after John Brown's Raid. The campaign had been stormy and sometimes violent. Moderate Democrat Thomas Overton Moore had been elected by the greatest majority in the state's history, 25,556 votes to 15,388 votes for Thomas J. Wells, and had carried every parish except Terrebonne. What would Louisiana's course of action be in the great crisis which confronted the nation? Her year of decision was about to begin.

II

1860—The Year of Decision

Governor Wickliffe's Last Message to the People of Louisiana.
Three months after John Brown's invasion of the South at Harpers
Ferry, the Louisiana Legislature met in regular session. The state
was tense, uneasy. Recent events were on every tongue—John
Brown's expedition, his trial and execution, the rising sympathy
toward Brown throughout the North, the bitter contest in Congress
over the selection of the Speaker of the House of Representatives.
The dissolution of the Union was not only a possibility but a probability of easy execution if the extremists of the North continued to
threaten the institution of slavery.

Retiring Governor Robert C. Wickliffe had planned to give but
little space to "national affairs" in his last Legislative message, but
the exigencies of the times forced major consideration upon "a dis-
agreeable topic." The North had waged sectional warfare upon the
South for a quarter century. The Northern abolitionist "fanatics"
had grown from "a mere speck upon the horizon" to a great cloud
which blackened "the skies of the majority section of the Confederacy." This force, which had defied the Constitution and the laws of
Congress, must be "confronted and beaten back." Louisiana held
firm, stood proudly against the flood, her character not yet "stained
with servility or dishonor."

Wickliffe condemned John Brown's Raid, saying that the "numbers actively engaged in it were insignificant; but when we take
into consideration that they committed the crimes of treason and
murder, and were provided to equip with arms for the work of
death, several thousand slaves or other confederates; that the general press and people of the extreme North, on various grounds,
sympathized with the traitors and murderers and solicited their
pardon, we cannot close our eyes to the inauspicious condition of
affairs." Few of Louisiana's citizens disagreed with the Governor.
Wickliffe recommended that the Legislature should give "a solemn
pledge that our State will stand by her sister Southern States to the
utmost extent of the men and means she can command, in any
course they may see proper to adopt to secure our Constitutional

rights." As Louisiana's share of the costs of securing these rights, he recommended that the Legislature appropriate $25,000.

Henry Watkins Allen of West Baton Rouge Parish, Chairman of the House Committee on Federal Relations, introduced a resolution condemning Brown's attempted insurrection as an attack upon the entire South and emphatically stating that the election of a Republican President in the fall election would warrant a "Southern Convention" and the secession of the Southern states. While extant records and the Louisiana Acts of 1860 do not reveal whether or not the Allen Resolutions were ever officially acted upon by the Legislature, the Governor was ordered to co-operate with the other Southern states "as the circumstances of the case and the honor of the country may require."

Beginning of Governor Moore's Administration. The new North Carolina–born Governor had migrated to Louisiana at the age of twenty-four and had become a Rapides Parish planter. He later served on the parish police jury and as a Democrat in the state Senate from 1856 to 1860. At the time of his inauguration on January 23, 1860, the Baton Rouge *Daily Gazette and Comet* expressed the opinion that "We are favorably impressed with Governor Moore's personal appearance. . . . We take him to be a gentleman of firmness and decision of character, and shall be very much deceived if the measure of our standard falls short."

In his inaugural address, Moore spoke of the general conservatism of Louisianians, for never in her history had the state "countenanced extreme opinions of violent measures." Her devotion to the Union was unquestioned, and if ever that devotion was weakened it would be because "intolerance has resulted in practical oppression or produced a state of things to which no sensitive people can submit." He regretted the rise of a purely sectional Republican party and believed that should it again gain control of the nation "the Southern States will be practically without representation in the Federal Government, and the South will occupy the position of subjugated states."

The new Governor deplored the rising spirit of disunion throughout the South and Louisiana: " . . . no man who has watched the course of the public mind can fail to have observed that in Louisiana, as in other Southern States, the progress of disunion feeling has been marked and rapid." He supported the state-rights position that "the Union cannot last without a recognition of the vital principles of the Constitution, that the States are equal in the Confederacy," and strongly emphasized that "every State must be permitted to determine her own social institutions, and left to the enjoyment of them in peace."

He made a final optimistic appeal in closing the address: "It is my belief, as well as my hope . . . that there will yet be allowed to all the States independence and equality, and that harmony and peace will be restored to our people without a sacrifice of interest or a loss of honor."

The Presidential Election of 1860. A little over a month and a half after the inauguration of Governor Moore, the State Democratic Convention met in Baton Rouge to select delegates to the national convention at Charleston, South Carolina. The "Old Liners" were in complete command, and the delegates were instructed to vote consistently as a unit for John C. Breckinridge of Kentucky and to support the Southern position regarding slavery. A resolution was passed recommending that in the event of a Republican victory, "Louisiana should meet in council with her sister slaveholding States to consult as to the means of future protection."

The national party conventions met in April and May, 1860. The Democratic party, after fifty-seven unsuccessful ballots, split into two groups; the Northern group met later at Baltimore and nominated Stephen A. Douglas of Illinois, the Southern group met at Richmond and selected John C. Breckinridge of Kentucky. The Republican party at its Chicago convention enthusiastically nominated Abraham Lincoln of Illinois and drafted a platform which appealed to the North and West, while the remnants of the old Whig and American parties organized the Constitutional Union party and nominated John Bell of Tennessee.

The presidential campaign in Louisiana was noisy, stirring, sometimes violent, and was characterized by flamboyant speeches, barbecues, parades, bands, ringing bells, waving banners and flags, and all the other implements of typical American political enthusiasms. Political clubs flourished—The Young Bell Ringers, The Young Men's Douglas Clubs, The Minute Men of '60, The Breckinridge Guards, and others. All the candidates except Lincoln had numerous backers who were extremely vocal in their loyal support and who gave money and time to the chosen leader.

While the Breckinridge supporters generally were less noisy than the followers of Douglas or Bell, the Guards organized local voter groups and campaigned in every community. Carefully organized rallies were spoken of as "having just happened spontaneously"; at one such Breckinridge affair in New Orleans, the press reported that "20,000 voices uprose in earnest plaudits in approval of his manly sentiments."

Bell supporters rang bells and chimes and sang "The Union Song" at every opportunity:

> Come boys, let's sing a song to-night,
> And ring the Bell with all our might,
>   Hurrah! Hurrah! Hurrah for the Union.

Union newspapers headlined: "Patriots of Louisiana! Patriots of the South! . . . The time is short—the emergency is pressing and vital; and the Union expects every man to discharge his whole duty. Do it, and earn the gratitude of your countrymen, and the blessing of your God." Christian Roselius, one of the most noted of the state's orators, keynoted his speeches: "Our Rights in the Union, if we can, out of the Union if we Must." But opponents cost Bell many

11

votes with their constant references of respect for the "quaint, homely, sleepy old gentleman."

Northern Democratic candidate Douglas had more followers than might have been expected, many backing him because they firmly believed that he was the only candidate who had a chance of beating Lincoln. Supporting newspapers admired him "for his bold, consistent and fearless course," and the Baton Rouge *Weekly Gazette and Comet* declared that he was "demanded by the largest and best half of the people." Pierre Soule believed that the election of any other candidate might mean the ruin "of that glorious fabric, the Constitution." But opponents called him "an egotistic worn-out political hack," argued that his ambition was "Rule or Ruin," and titled him "the Illinois Traitor."

As for Lincoln, it is doubtful that he had a hundred passive supporters throughout the entire state, but there was much vocal and printed opposition to him just the same. The objectives of Lincoln and the "Black Republicans" were simple: " . . . not only the political subjugation but the social ruin and destruction of the people of the Southern states." Judah P. Benjamin, in comparing Lincoln and Douglas, said: "I have no stomach for a fight in which I am to have the choice between the man who denies me all my rights, openly and fairly [Lincoln], and a man who admits my rights but intends to filch them [Douglas]." To the New Orleans *Crescent*, Lincoln was simply "the dirtiest and meanest Abolitionist alive."

So the days of summer passed, with campaign tensions gripping the people of Louisiana. But, politically excited though they were, they were still Americans and stopped campaigning long enough to properly celebrate the Fourth of July. J. W. Dorr reported the celebration at Natchitoches: "The enthusiastic citizens have cleared out the muzzle of the antique six pounder which frowns savagely down the empty bed of Cane river in front of the city, and there will be burning of powder, making of speeches and eating and drinking, and barbecuing and blowing of horns, and sore heads and repentance next day. Hooray for the Fourth of July! Hooray South and North! There, that's my celebration. . . ."

During the last month of the campaign a sort of dread seriousness spread over the entire state. On October 6, John Slidell published an address to his "Fellow-Citizens of Louisiana" in which he prophetically said: "Let every man go to the polls with a deep sense of the importance of this election. Let him cast his vote conscientiously for the candidate to whom he may consider it safest to confide our destinies for the next four years, but let him do so without any bitterness toward his neighbor, who may differ from him, for they may, perhaps, soon be called on to act together under a common flag and against common enemies."

Abraham Lincoln was elected President but received less than 40 per cent of the total national popular vote. Breckinridge received majorities in central and northern Louisiana, his vote totaling 22,681, while Bell and Douglas were strongest in the southern plantation sections and in New Orleans, their support totaling 20,204 and 7,625 votes respectively. The two conservative tickets were in great majority and ran very close races in seven parishes. Abraham Lincoln, not having an electorial ticket, did not receive a single vote.

A Dramatic Month. The month from the November 7 election day to the meeting of the Special Session of the Legislature on December 10 was a month of continued political arguments and heart-searching over the questions of state rights, slavery, the possible future courses of action of the Republican party and its President-elect, and the future position of Louisiana in the Union. Governor Moore stated that while he would try to preserve the Union, he would recommend a conference of all the Southern states. "The Southern Rights Association of the State of Louisiana" was organized, with a platform of "Southern Rights, Southern honor, Southern Independence"; and branches sprang up over the entire state. On November 11, John Slidell wrote to President James Buchanan that Governor Moore would probably convene the Legislature at an early date and that Louisiana would act with her "sister States of the South"; he saw no possibility of preserving the Union.

Newspaper reaction to the election of Lincoln was sharply divided. The conservative press, led by the New Orleans *Daily True Delta,* the New Orleans *Picayune,* and the Baton Rouge *Gazette and Comet,* called for coolheaded leadership, moderation, and slow deliberation on the problems facing the nation. On November 8, the day after the election, the New Orleans *Bee* urged that "it will be time to fight Lincoln with gunpowder and the sword, when we find either that constitutional resistance fails, or that he and his party are bent on our humiliation and destruction. We are for the Union so long as it is possible to preserve it. . . . Hence we say again, *let us wait.*" A month later the *Picayune* pledged that "where our state finally goes, we are prepared to go, but until she acts, we shall labor to show all the difficulties, all the dangers, of following mere impulses instead of being guided by great principles."

Less conservative sheets like the New Orleans *Crescent* took the position that Union at any price was too dear and favored both state and Southern conventions. One paper summed up their general position: " . . . we are secessionists because we honestly believe that it is the only possible way in which we can enjoy the rights and privileges which the Union, as originally designed, was intended to bestow upon all the States, according to the just measure of Equality."

A few newspapers attempted to break the tension with humorous sallies, as for example did the Alexandria *Constitutional* when it printed: "If Louisiana secedes from the Union . . . we shall be compelled to advocate the secession of the parish of Rapides from

13

the State. . . . We have a large territory and a numerous population and we are perfectly able to take care of ourselves."

On November 19, the Governor called for a special session of the Legislature, because of the election of Lincoln "by a sectional and aggressive anti-slavery party, whose hostility to the people and institutions of the South has been evidenced by repeated and long-continued violations of Constitutional obligations and fraternal amity" and because "the necessity for self-preservation requires us to deliberate upon our own course of action."

Ten days later, Bishop B. M. Palmer of the First Presbyterian Church of New Orleans preached a Thanksgiving Day sermon which was to have tremendous significance throughout the state in determining popular public opinion on the secession question. He denounced Abolitionists, explained the Southern defense of slavery, argued that the South should stand her ground and if necessary secede from the Federal Union, and gave the Southern promise that "though war be the aggregation of all evils, yet should the madness of the hour appeal to the arbitration of the sword, we will not shrink even from the baptism of fire." In closing, with terrifying intensity and deep feeling, he said: "Whatever be the fortunes of the South, I accept them for my own. Born upon her soil . . . she is in every sense my mother. I shall die upon her bosom—she shall know no peril, but it is my peril—no conflict, but it is my conflict —and no abyss or ruin, into which I shall not share her fall. May the Lord God cover her head in this her day of battle."

The audience sat still—an eternity compressed into a few brief moments—then filed slowly from the church. One witness later wrote: "After the benediction, in solemn silence, no man speaking to his neighbor, the great congregation of serious and thoughtful men and women dispersed; but afterwards the drums beat and the bugles sounded; for New Orleans was shouting for secession."

The sermon was printed by the newspapers, and then in pamphlet form, of which 30,000 copies were soon sold. Few citizens challenged Bishop Palmer, but the New Orleans *Daily True Delta* questioned: "You would destroy the Constitution and the Union—this glorious and peerless fabric which has so long and so safely sheltered us, and what, sir, would you rear in its stead?" But Palmer's words caused many Louisianians to decide that there could only be co-operation with a North which truly desired to co-operate with the South—or secession.

. . *The Special Session of the Legislature.* The Special Session of the Legislature met at the capitol from December 10 to 12. The deliberations of the sixty-one Representatives and twenty-three Senators present were marked by general harmony. The Governor's message emphasized that the time had passed when men hesitated to calculate the value of the Federal Union. He recommended the calling of a state convention to determine the future position of Louisiana in that Union. He also maintained that each state had the constitu-

14

tional right of secession, and that should the states of the South secede and any attempt "be made by the Federal government to coerce a sovereign state, and compel her to submit to an authority which she has ceased to recognize, I should unhesitatingly recommend that Louisiana assist her sister states."

Following the Governor's leadership, the Legislature passed four acts relative to Louisiana's future position in the Union: the Governor was ordered to call a special election to be held on January 7, 1861, for delegates to a state convention which would meet at Baton Rouge on January 23; $25,000 was appropriated to pay the costs of the convention; $500,000 was appropriated for military purposes; and the Governor was requested to communicate with the governors of the Southern states "in relation to the present critical condition of the country." Just before adjournment a resolution was passed which emphasized that "any attempt to coerce or force a sovereign State to remain within the Union . . . will be viewed by the people of Louisiana . . . as a hostile invasion and resisted to the utmost."

At the Year's End. The winter of 1860–61 in the South's winter capital of New Orleans promised to be even gayer than usual. The drawing rooms and salons of the principal hotels were crowded with planters and businessmen and their families. Adelina Patti was headlining an opera season, the brilliance of which the old city had never seen. But an intense excitement was in the air. Everyone talked politics—what course of action would the Southern states take before the inauguration of Abraham Lincoln.

Enthusiasms ran high, As one lady wrote in her "memories": "Who does not remember the epidemic of blue cockades which broke out in New Orleans during the winter of 1860 and 1861, and raged violently throughout the whole city? The little blue cockade, with its pelican button in the centre and its two small streamers, was the distinguishing mark of the 'Secessionist.' " On December 15, the *Weekly Delta* said that "Governor Moore is not what may be called a 'fast man' in politics; but if he is slower than some others, he is just as sure to come right in the end." On the twenty-fourth, Sallie Holman, member of a theatrical troupe, introduced "The Southern Marseillaise," a new song which pleaded for the South to "awake to glory!" At the year's closing another new song called "Dixie" had been "adopted" by New Orleanians, who were thrilling to the words: "In Dixie Land we'll take our stand, to lib an' die in Dixie."

With the last days of December, Louisianians became quiet and serious. Few of them now questioned the "right" of secession; the Federal Union had preceded the Constitution and the national government—the states had the right to leave that Union just as they had joined it, by individual state action. Most Louisianians had wrestled in their Gethsemane and had allied themselves with one of two groups, the "Immediate Secessionists," who believed that Louisiana should immediately leave the Union, and the "Co-operationists," who believed that the state should co-operate with the other Southern states and delay action until President-elect Lincoln had assumed office and had announced his policies.

The year 1860 had been the year of decision; 1861 would be the year of action.

III

Secession and the Republic of Louisiana

Secession or Co-operation? Louisianians had known many dramatic years during the eight-score years of their history, but none more dramatic than 1860. During those twelve months, Louisianians had studied and discussed, argued and debated, contemplated and prayed, and in the last weeks had reached an almost unanimous decision that a state had the constitutional right to secede from the Federal Union, and that it then had the right to organize as an independent nation or to join with other states in the formation of a new union. The major question, then, on January 1, 1861, was the expediency of secession. Should Louisiana secede from the Union at this time, as South Carolina had already done, or should it remain in the Union and attempt to co-operate with the incoming Lincoln government in the hope that the difficulties between North and South could be settled? On this question the people were sharply and rather evenly divided.

The Special Election of Delegates to a State Convention. The campaign for the election of delegates to the State Convention had taken on the proportions of a regular political campaign, with rallies, parades, newspaper headlines, decorations, bands, and the constant waving of the Pelican Flag. The news that South Carolina had seceded was received in New Orleans on December 21 with wildly enthusiastic demonstrations and the firing of 800 guns. For twenty-five years Abolitionists had heaped tar and pitch upon the flames of Northern antislavery sectionalism; now Southern extremists hurled lighted torches over the land south of Mason and Dixon's line.

Louisiana secessionists believed that the election of the Republican candidate made it impossible to protect the Southern social and economic system within the framework of the Constitution. In October, 1860, in a Leavenworth, Kansas, campaign speech, Lincoln had said that "if constitutionally we elect a president, and therefore you undertake to destroy the Union, it will be our duty to deal with you as old John Brown was dealt with. We can only do our duty." On November 21, the Indianapolis *Indiana American* had thundered: *"Our voice is for war!* If it be bloody, fierce and devastating, be it so." Ten days later the Chicago *Daily Democrat* had forcefully summarized the Northern position: "You have sworn that if we dared to elect such a man [President-elect Lincoln] you would dissolve the Union. We have elected him, and now we want you to try your little game of secession. Do it, if you dare. . . . But every man of you who attempts to subvert this Union . . . will be hung as high as Heaven. We will have no fooling about this matter. By the eternal! the Union must be preserved."

Southern political leaders also were not reticent in expressing their views. Senator Louis T. Wigfall of Texas, for example, in a December speech in the Senate roared that the next American treaty would be signed between the North and South at Faneuil Hall in Boston. Louisiana Senators John Slidell and Judah P. Benjamin and Representatives John M. Landrum and Thomas G. Davidson strongly favored secession but did not express their opinions in as vehement language as had the Senator from Texas. Other secessionist leaders included J. D. B. De Bow, noted editor of *De Bow's Review*, Charles Gayarré, historian and former Louisiana Secretary of State, Bishop B. M. Palmer, and Governor Thomas Overton Moore. On the other side, the co-operationists were led by former Governor A. B. Roman, former senator and former minister to Spain Pierre Soule, Catahoula Parish political leader James G. Taliaferro, and Orleans Parish leaders Christian Roselius, Joseph A. Rozier, and Randall Hunt.

By January 7 many people had lost interest in the campaign. They believed that the great majority of Louisianians favored secession and so did not go to the polls. Only 37,744 voted, whereas over 50,000 had cast their ballots in the preceding presidential election. Twenty-nine parishes favored secession; 19 were opposed. The vote in New Orleans was 4,358 for secession and 3,978 for co-operation. But there was no real state-wide pattern, for of the 19 co-operationist parishes, 11 were in the southeastern section of the state and 8 in the northern. To the State Convention would go 80 delegates pledged to support secession, 44 pledged for co-operation with the Federal government, and 6 who were undecided.

Louisianians who favored immediate secession were elated; those who believed in co-operation looked with foreboding at the future. University of Louisiana law student E. John Ellis of Amite wrote to his father that all was gone except hope, "I can see nothing before us but a long bloody war. I do not doubt the chivalry of Southern men, but reason & common sense forces the conviction upon me that in a conflict between the sections the North would over-match us. . . . If it comes to the worst, as Southerners we must fight to the last man."

Superintendent William T. Sherman of the State Seminary of Learning and Military Academy sent his letter of resignation to Governor Moore on January 18, writing that "if Louisiana withdraws from the Federal Union, I prefer to maintain my allegiance to the Constitution as long as a fragment of it survives." On his last day at the institution he ordered the battalion of students formed, made a brief talk, and then walked down the lines, shaking hands, patting a shoulder, straightening a collar, while tears rolled down the cheeks of the cadets. Then, turning to the little group of professors, according to David French Boyd, who later became president of the institution, "he silently shook our hands, attempted to speak, broke down, and, with his eyes filled with tears, with another effort, he could only lay his hand on his heart and say: 'you are all here.' Then, turning quickly on his heel, he left us, to be ever in our hearts."

The Louisiana State Convention of 1861. The State Convention of 1861 met in its first session at the capitol in Baton Rouge from January 23 to January 26.* Of the 130 elected members 127 were present. Effingham Lawrence of Plaquemines Parish called the Convention to order and then asked John Perkins, Jr., senatorial delegate from the parishes of Madison, Tensas, and Concordia, to take the chair. A temporary secretary, assistant secretary, and sergeant-at-arms were appointed.

The roll call revealed that it was a middle-aged group, averaging 42.5 years; 23 delegates were over 50 and 7 under 30. The youngest delegate was 21-year-old David Pierson of Winn Parish, while the eldest was 73-year-old Thomas W. Scott of East Feliciana. Forty-seven members were native-born Louisianians, 9 had been born in foreign countries, 11 were natives of the North, and the rest were from the other states of the South. Seventy-five members were planters, farmers, or owned agricultural land. Other occupational groups included 39 lawyers, 7 public officials, 5 doctors, and 2 editors; one delegate listed his occupation as "omnibus," and another as an "adjuster of averages." Collectively, 107 of them owned a total of 6,016 slaves; 19 delegates each owned 100 or more and 36 owned more than 50.

After the roll call, former Governor Alexandre Mouton was elected president of the body. In a short address he stated that he expected the sessions to be marked by "calmness and deliberation," for "we are engaged in an important cause, the cause of a brave, loyal and enlightened people asserting their rights. . . ." Commissioners from South Carolina and Alabama were invited to seats on the floor of the Convention and several committees were appointed, one of them a fifteen-member committee "whose object is to draw

* The original manuscript journal of the Convention, a volume of several hundred pages, was stolen from the state capitol by a Federal soldier during the occupation of Baton Rouge. It was later acquired by a Rhode Island officer whose son returned it to the state in 1929. It is now in the Louisiana State Museum at New Orleans. The printed journal, the *Official Journal of the Proceedings of the Convention of the State of Louisiana* (New Orleans: J. O. Nixon, Printer to the State Convention, 1861), is exceptionally rare, and was therefore facsimile-printed in the Winter, 1961 (Volume II, Number 1), issue of *Louisiana History*, the official publication of the Louisiana Historical Association.

an ordinance providing for the withdrawal of the State of Louisiana from the present Federal Union."

Chairman John Perkins, Jr., of the Committee of Fifteen, presented on January 24 the committee's report, "An Ordinance to Dissolve the Union between the State of Louisiana and other States united with her, under the compact entitled 'The Constitution of the United States.'" * Joseph A. Rozier and James O. Fuqua offered substitute ordinances. Governor Moore reported that he had taken possession of the United States military barracks and arsenal at Baton Rouge and Forts Pike, Jackson, and St. Philip. A motion to approve the Governor's action passed 119 to 5.

Eleven standing committees were appointed on January 25, additional convention officials were announced, and a communication from the Louisiana congressional delegation was read. Chairman John Perkins, Jr., of the Committee of Fifteen attempted to call up his committee's "Ordinance of Secession," but the Rozier substitute ordinance was considered instead and failed of passage by a vote of 106 to 24. At an evening meeting, Fuqua's substitute ordinance also lost, 73 to 47.

On Saturday, January 26, after the Convention had decided to move to New Orleans on January 29, a resolution by Charles Bienvenu to "refer the action of this Convention on the Ordinance of Secession to the people" was killed by a vote of 84 to 43. The Ordinance of Secession was now called up and a recess of twenty minutes granted at the request of John L. Lewis of Claiborne Parish.

On the return of the delegates to their seats about one o'clock, several members, led by James G. Taliaferro of Catahoula Parish, spoke in opposition to the Ordinance of Secession.† Taliaferro gave the following reasons for his opposition:

1. The acts of aggression against the State could be remedied under the United States Constitution.
2. If the State did secede it would not remedy matters.
3. There was a possibility that the seceded states would not confederate or that the border slave states would secede.

* During the late 1930's this writer, at that time head of the Department of Archives of Louisiana State University and engaged in collecting state historical, manuscript, and archival material for the Department, found the lost original draft of the secession ordinance with a group of "worthless" papers in the home of Lemuel P. Conner, Jr., of Natchez, Mississippi. Conner's father, who had lived in Louisiana and who was a member of the Convention, was a close friend of John Perkins, Jr. They spent the night of January 23 writing and revising a draft of a secession ordinance which Perkins presented to his Committee of Fifteen the following morning. The final draft of the Louisiana secession ordinance is essentially the same as Perkins and Conner wrote it. Perkins kept the original draft and sent it to Conner shortly before his death in Baltimore in 1885. The Conner family still has possession of the historic document, and photostats are in the Department of Archives, Louisiana State University.

† The *Official Journal* did not list the speakers nor give any information regarding their arguments.

4. Secession was a right not contemplated by the Constitution of the United States.
5. The proper status of Louisiana was with the border states.
6. By secession the State of Louisiana lost any claim it had to the public domain and to all property belonging to the Union.
7. Secession would produce hardships, suffering, and destruction of property.
8. The Ordinance of Secession had been drawn by a convention which did not possess the legal right to sever relations with the Union.

The Ordinance of Secession was then adopted by a vote of 113 to 17, Convention President Mouton being permitted to vote through a suspension of the rules. When the result of the vote was revealed, President Mouton proclaimed: "In virtue of the vote just announced, I now declare the connection between the State of Louisiana and the Federal Union dissolved, and that she is a free, sovereign, and independent power." The bar of the house was removed, "and His Excellency, Thomas O. Moore, Governor of the Independent State of Louisiana, entered upon the floor, preceded by the Flag of the State, and took position on the platform of the President." The Reverend W. E. N. Lingfield offered a prayer and Father Darius Hubert blessed the flag. Later, when the Ordinance was officially signed by the Convention members, 8 of the 17 members who had voted against it signed the document, making the final vote 121 to 9.

Upon receiving official copies of the Ordinance of Secession, Louisiana Senators Judah P. Benjamin and John Slidell, and three of the four Representatives, Thomas G. Davidson, John M. Landrum, and Miles Taylor, departed for home. Slidell defended the right of secession with militant spirit; Benjamin was more moderate but argued the legal right of revolution, admitted that Louisianians were traitors just as was Patrick Henry and that they had committed "just such treason as encircles with a sacred halo the undying name of Washington." However, Louisiana Representative John E. Bouligny, who had been elected to Congress as a "National American," did not resign his seat. He was the only representative from a seceding state to remain in Washington after the beginning of hostilities. He died at his post in 1864.

For Louisiana the deed was done. Like the other Southern states, she would face four years of war and twelve years of military occupation afterward; but, along with her sister commonwealths, she would never in the years to come apologize for secession.

The people of the state generally received the news with sincere approval and celebrated Louisiana's independence with enthusiastic spontaneity; guns banged, cannons thundered, state flags were flung to the breeze, and at night public buildings and private homes were brightly lighted. Everyone was ready to "defend the sovereignty of Louisiana," according to the *Picayune,* and "every-

21

one's heart beat with a more pleasurable pulsation." The New Orleans *Crescent* editorialized that the state had escaped "from a Union in which she could no longer remain with honor to herself or to her sister states of the South." The Shreveport *South-Western* sadly admitted: "It is with heart-felt emotions . . . that we fold the saucy looking 'star spangled banner' that we have always loved, and place the precious memento under our pillow."

The "Republic" of Louisiana. For almost two months, from January 26 to March 21 when she became a member of the Confederate States of America, Louisiana was an independent nation. Governor Moore acted as president, the Legislature continued in session as a congress, and the state courts served as federal courts.

The old state flag was used as a national flag until February 11, when a new emblem was adopted by the Convention. The new flag had thirteen red, white, and blue stripes and in the upper left-hand corner a five-pointed yellow star in a red field. The flag represented the thirteen original states, the French tricolor, and the red and yellow colors of Spain. At eleven o'clock on the morning of February 12, the members of the Convention, headed by Alexandre Mouton and Lieutenant Governor Henry M. Hyams, marched to Lafayette Square. The flag, made by tentmaker and sailmaker H. Cassidy, was raised over the City Hall, and received a twenty-one-gun salute from the Washington Artillery. Here it flew until pulled down by Federal soldiers after the occupation of New Orleans in 1862.

By the middle of February, 1861, Governor Moore had taken possession of all Federal property in Louisiana, including the Mint and Customs House in New Orleans along with over $600,000 in the Mint. The Convention, which held its second and third sessions in New Orleans, and the "Louisiana National Congress" (Legislature) continued to meet, the "Congress" passing laws and the Convention adopting ordinances. The work of the Convention was of more significance and it performed functions which were actually the prerogative of the "Congress." It transferred the powers of the United States government to the new Louisiana national government and directed financial, judicial, and postal affairs. Meanwhile the "Congress" appropriated $1,500,000 for the defense of the new nation, provided for the organization of military forces, and outfitted warships at the Algiers shipyard.

While there was some criticism of the Convention's continuing its activities after the passage of the Ordinance of Secession, the majority of its members and the people of the state believed that it was only performing functions "imperatively demanded by the withdrawal of the State from the Union."

Had secession been the proper course of action? The editor of the New Orleans *Bee* wrote that "the secession movement . . . grew too fast . . . to warrant the faintest hope of retarding its progress. . . . All that could be done by moderate, dispassionate, political and experienced men was to go with the current, endeavoring to subdue its boiling and seething energies." A majority of Louisianians, however, would probably have agreed with Northern Bishop Thomas M. Clark, who, in a letter to Mrs. Leonidas Polk after the war, discussed the bitter condemnation in the North of her bishop husband for his decision to fight for the South. Bishop Clark wrote: "I was well persuaded that he regarded his course as a sacrifice laid on the altar of truth, and went forth believing himself to be called to wield the sword of the Lord and of Gideon."

Louisiana Joins the Confederate States of America. On January 29, when the Convention began holding its meetings in New Orleans, six delegates were selected, two from the state at large and one from each congressional district, to represent Louisiana at "the Convention of seceding States proposed to be held at Montgomery [Alabama] . . . on the fourth day of February, 1861." The delegates were John Perkins, Jr., Alexander Declouet, Charles M. Conrad, Duncan F. Kenner, Henry Marshall, and Edward Sparrow.

The delegates from the six Southern states which had seceded— South Carolina, Mississippi, Florida, Alabama, Georgia, and Louisiana—met at Montgomery on the appointed day. The Southern delegates, as Charles P. Roland has written, "were driven by a great sense of urgency to get the provisional government into operation with utmost speed and with a minimum of controversy." Jefferson Davis of Mississippi was unanimously elected provisional president of the Confederate States of America and Alexander H. Stephens of Georgia was chosen provisional vice-president.

The organization of the Southern Confederacy was enthusiastically hailed throughout the state, except by a few vocal co-operationists. Joseph A. Rozier favored a new convention, for secession had been a "hasty action," while Christian Roselius believed that the Montgomery Convention had "dug the grave of American Liberty."

On February 11, President-elect Lincoln left Springfield, Illinois, for the national capital, facing, as he said, "a task before me greater than that which rested upon Washington." In his inaugural address on March 4 he was firm but conciliatory toward the South; he would not interfere with slavery where it already existed, but "Physically speaking, we cannot separate. . . . No State, upon its own mere action, can lawfully get out of the Union." With those words Lincoln revealed that the North would not permit the "erring Southern Sisters" to depart from the old Union in peace. Student John Ellis' forebodings of "a long bloody war" would come to pass.

The Convention, which had adjourned on February 12, reassembled on March 4. On March 19 it received the Constitution of the Confederate States, which had been passed a week earlier, and two days later began consideration of the document. Several attempts were made by co-operationist delegates to submit the constitution to a special convention or to the people, but each such move was

23

decisively defeated. Finally on the twenty-first, Daniel O'Bryan of Vermilion Parish presented "AN ORDINANCE providing for the approval and ratification of the Constitution of the Confederate States of America." After several delaying attempts, a substitute ordinance by Thomas J. Semmes of New Orleans was passed 100 to 7. The Confederate constitution was entered in the *Official Journal* on March 23.

Before it finally adjourned on March 26, the Convention officially approved the "Stars and Bars" flag of the Confederacy. Now Louisianians and Southerners, like Northerners with their Stars and Stripes, took their "Banner of the Bars" and nailed it just below the Cross.

. .*The War Begins.* Both nations rapidly began to mobilize for war, for the issue was now "victory or subjugation . . . the recognition or total destruction of the institutions of the South." At 4:30 A.M. on April 12, 1861, Confederate shore batteries under command of Louisiana's Pierre G. T. Beauregard opened fire on Fort Sumter, which was on an island in the bay off Charleston, South Carolina. The fort surrendered after thirty-four hours of bombardment. On April 15, President Lincoln called for 75,000 volunteers to force the South back into the Federal fold, insisting that his "paramount object" was "to save the Union."

On April 19, the Sixth Massachusetts Regiment, passing through Baltimore on its way southward, in a fight with the citizens killed twelve and wounded a number of others. The New Orleans *Daily Crescent* screamed the headline the following morning: "Northern Troops Moving Southward—They are Attacked by the Baltimoreans." The news spread rapidly by telegraph and river packet throughout Louisiana.

Twenty-five-year-old James Ryder Randall, Maryland-born but with Louisiana family connections, a Pointe Coupee Parish, Poydras College teacher, was at the New Roads Mississippi River wharf when the news arrived. Unable to sleep that night, he arose, lighted a candle, seized his pen, and wrote the words to one of the most stirring and beloved songs of the Confederacy:

> The despot's heel is on thy shore
> His torch is at thy temple door
>
> . . . .
> Thou wilt not yield the vandal toll
> Thou wilt not crook to his control
> Better the fire upon thee roll,
> Better the shot, the blade, the bowl,
> Than crucifixion of the soul,
>   Maryland, my Maryland!

A few days later the conservative Alexandria *Constitutional* heralded the new union of Southern states: "There is but one voice in the land, one purpose, one heart, and one destiny." Young Kate Stone wrote in her diary that "Our Cause is just and must prevail."

Donelson Caffery later said in the United States Senate: "I revered the Union and I honored its flag. But when my state called me to arms, I had to answer the call of the state of my nativity and the state of my love."

The Southern soul searchings had ended. The prayers had been said. The campaigns and the elections, the conventions and the speechmaking were over. It was now time for the bloody work of war.

IV

1861—Louisiana Mobilizes for War

Louisiana and the War. The War for Southern Independence may or may not have been inevitable, but almost from the beginning of the secession movement in the South many Northern and Southern political leaders predicted that there would be war between the two sections. With the organization of the Confederate States of America, the incoming President of the United States was placed upon the horns of a dilemma—he could either permit that new nation of confederated Southern states to become a nation in fact or he could apply the total manpower and physical resources of the United States to force the seceded states back into the old Union. That he chose the latter course is a matter of history.

Louisiana sent thousands of her soldiers to the war theaters east of the Mississippi and enlisted other thousands who fought in the trans-Mississippi area. Within the state there would be the long waiting and maneuvering of troops, the rapid raids and quick strikes of small units rather than major-objective campaigns and hard-fought, decisive battles between large armies. Only one important field campaign would be fought, that of the Red River in 1864, and only one significant defensive siege would be withstood, that heroic stand behind the earthen ramparts of Port Hudson, but the dozens of small engagements would be short, bloody melees where saber, shot, and shell would be the broad-cutting scythes of Mars.

Military and Economic Mobilization. During the long weeks and months of 1861, Louisianians prepared to fight. Early that year the state acquired over thirty cannon, nearly fifty thousand small arms, and a considerable quantity of ammunition and gunpowder through the capture of the Federal arsenal at Baton Rouge, and during the two-month period of independent nationality made rapid progress in the mobilization of her manpower and physical resources. Her efforts were redoubled after she joined the Confederacy.

A Military Board established by the Legislature in December, 1860, reported in February that each parish had been made a military district and that all white male citizens between the ages of

26

eighteen and fifty-five years were subject to "active" or "sedentary" militia duty. Company officers below the rank of captain would be elected by company members; captains and officers above that rank would be appointed by the Governor. The Board had already furnished arms to twenty-eight companies with a total enrollment of nearly 1,800 men. About the same time, a regular state military force, composed of one infantry regiment and an artillery regiment, under the control of the Governor, was established.

During this period military supplies of all types were deposited in government warehouses located at strategic points throughout the state. Boats collected scrap iron along the rivers and bayous and delivered it to iron foundries in New Orleans. Small industrial plants were built, converted, or enlarged to manufacture uniforms, hats, shoes, tents, and military equipment and munitions. The planting of corn and other food crops rather than such staples as cotton, tobacco, or even sugar cane was encouraged. At its November, 1861, session the Legislature passed general emergency laws and made appropriations for additional military equipment and supplies.

The Confederate States government asked the Governor for 1,700 troops on March 9 and a month later for an additional 3,000. On the day after Lincoln's appeal for 75,000 United States volunteers, Jefferson Davis asked for 32,000 troops from the Confederacy, Louisiana's quota of 5,000 men to be held "in readiness for instant movement."

By the first of June, 16,000 Louisianians were under arms; by the end of the year the number had risen to approximately 25,000. Parishes frequently exceeded their quotas. For example, 520 men from a total of 851 voters in Carroll Parish enlisted, and it was reported that "of the 1300 voters at Baton Rouge, more than 750 are already off to the wars."

Louisiana units began leaving their home-parish headquarters early in the spring, entraining or embarking for New Orleans, for Camp Moore near Amite, or for Mississippi River ports. On April 16 the Caddo Greys left Shreveport on the steamboat *Louis D'Or* for New Orleans and were followed the next day by the Caddo Rifles on the *Grand Duke*. "The levee was crowded with ladies, gentlemen and children," wrote the *Daily News*, "anxious to have another look at the brave defenders of our rights. As the boat left the shore, the band of the Caddo Rifles struck up a very appropriate tune—'The Girl I Left Behind Me'—and the cannon was made to belch forth its thundering sound. There was waving of handkerchiefs by ladies, tears tracing down smiling faces." The Hunter Rifles left Clinton for New Orleans on April 28, aboard "the cars" to Port Hudson, "all in a high glee and as we had some violins aboard, they were fiddling and dancing all the way down."

The first troops to leave the state, four companies of Zouaves under the command of Major Waldemar Hyllested and Captain Al-

27

fred Coppens, left New Orleans on March 29 to join the Confederate forces at Pensacola. The First Louisiana Regulars and the Orleans Cadets, under Captain Charles D. Dreux, who would be the first Louisiana soldier killed in the war,* left on April 11 and were followed within a few days by the Caddo Greys, the Crescent Rifles, the Louisiana Guards, and the Washington Artillery.

On the Sunday before their departure the members of the Washington Artillery assembled in uniform at Christ Church to hear a sermon by the Reverend Doctor W. T. Leacock, many of the men going through the forms of the Episcopal service with the clang of their sabers "echoing through the solemn vaulted aisles." The next day the 300 men marched through "surging crowds" to the railroad station and one of them later wrote that "distinctions of society, wealth, and station were forgotten, and each departing soldier was equally honored as a hero." Altogether over 980 companies were organized in Louisiana during the course of the war, and many of their departures compared with that of the noted New Orleans artillery battalion.

Public Enthusiasm. By this time, according to the *Picayune*, New Orleans had assumed a "most warlike and military appearance. . . . The wildest military enthusiasm and patriotism prevails." The Confederate flag flew from public and private buildings, bands blared, military companies paraded, and William H. Russell reported that "the streets are full of Turcos, Zouaves, Chasseurs . . . there are Pickwick Rifles, LaFayette, Beauregard, MacMahon guards. . . . In fact, New Orleans looks like a suburb of the camp at Chalons."

The scene was much the same over the entire state, as, according to a Baton Rouge paper, "the enthusiasm of the people . . . begins to rise." In Plaquemine the talk was war, "nothing but war." In northeast Louisiana, Jack Myers was one of "a little band of patriotic and gallant young men" who "started to Girard where they could take the cars next day for New Orleans." In Thibodaux, Winchester Hall closed his law office, went to an enlistment barbecue, and helped organize the Allen Rifles, of which he became the first lieutenant. Everyone "tried to join up at once," and there were more volunteers than the state could equip.

John S. Kendall wrote later that he "shared the popular delusion that the war would last only a short time," and "that unless I got to the front at once, the fighting would all be over before I had a chance to take part in it." Many people believed that "the affair" would be "settled in ninety days," while numerous others strongly maintained that there would be no war at all, because "the North will not fight."

A large percentage of Louisiana's citizens were foreign born, had come from the states of the North, or had supported unionism rather than secession. The great majority of these groups, however,

* Captain Dreux was killed on July 5, 1861, at the Battle of Curtis' Farm, near Newport News, Virginia.

supported the state and the South when the war came. Unionist John S. Scott of Bayou Sara became colonel of the First Louisiana Cavalry and Maine-born Captain Arthur McArthur of the Sabine Rifles was killed at the Battle of Winchester, his Union-officer brother burying his body. Many of the foreign-born citizens became enthusiastic recruiters. The Irish were particularly vocal, and a number of them cruised the streets, collared less-enthusiastic Spaniards, and shouted, "For the love of the Virgin and your own sowl's sake, Fernandey, get up and cum along wid us to fight the Yankees." But many of the newly arrived citizens of New Orleans were undoubtedly driven to enlistment by economic necessity engendered by the blockade.

Most Louisianians lived during those stirring days of 1861 with their feet planted firmly in the clouds; others, just as patriotic, understood the forces of grim reality. But all were resolute. Teenager Kate Stone wrote that "throughout the length and breadth of the land the trumpet of war is sounding, and from every hamlet and village, from city and country, men are hurrying by thousands, eager to be led to battle against Lincoln's hordes. Bravely, cheerily they go, willing to meet death in defense of the South." Bishop Leonidas Polk wrote to his wife: "All are agreed now. There are not two parties any more. . . . Of the issue I have no doubt." William H. Russell reported that "As one looks at the resolute, quick, angry faces around him, and hears but the single theme, he must feel the South will never yield to the North, unless as a nation which is beaten beneath the feet of a victorious enemy." In September, Harry McCarthy sang his new composition "The Bonnie Blue Flag," at the New Orleans Academy of Music, and the enthusiasm of the audience grew into a riot of major proportions.

But all was not just wild, unthinking enthusiasm. The great majority of Louisianians soberly approved the course of action taken by their elected representatives and they strongly believed in the justice of their cause. They would have endorsed emphatically the statement which General Richard Taylor would write the day before Lee's surrender four years in the future: "The cause for which we have struggled for four years was a just one at the beginning of the war and it is just now."

Troops and Training Camps. Louisiana's enlistees quickly changed from civilians to soldiers. Volunteer companies drilled and paraded in every city, town, and village. The names given the new companies reflected local pride and group enthusiasm, and were often picturesque, including such titles as the Alligator Rangers, Calcasieu Tigers, Caddo Lake Boys, Chasseurs de la Fourche, Catahoula Guerillas, Cazadores Espanoles, Stars of Equality, De Soto Creoles, Knights of the Border, Hussars of the Teche, Mounted Wild Cats, Red River Sharpshooters, Slavonian Rifles, La Bisque Battery, West Feliciana Home Scouts, Sabine Independents, Madison Tipperarys, Yankee Pelters, Franklinton Pumpkin Studs, Yellow Jack Battalion, and numerous others equally individualistic.

Some of the companies were almost immediately sent to one of several training camps in the vicinity of New Orleans—Camp Lewis at Greenville Park, near Carrollton, Camp Walker at the Metairie Race Course, Camp Roman a short distance above Carrollton. Smaller camps were established at City Park, the Union Race Course, Lake End, and at the Jefferson City Gardens on the Carrollton Railroad. For a time, a camp near Clinton was occupied by companies of infantry, but it was not long before Camp Moore, on the Jackson Railroad north of New Orleans near Tangipahoa, became the most important training ground.

Most soldiers outfitted themselves with a uniform the style, cut, and color of which varied with the individual tastes of the company officers; arms and other equipment were usually supplied locally by company benefactors or by the state. Brightly colored and picturesque uniforms were much in evidence, and while most of them were of cheap cloth and inexpensively made, a few organizations, as for example the Crescent Cadets and the Washington Artillery, wore tailor-made uniforms of the finest imported materials.

Upon his enlistment or the organization of a company, the prospective soldier took the oath of allegiance to the State of Louisiana; later the oath included loyalty to the Confederacy. He gave his age, birthplace, height, and color of complexion, hair, and eyes, and agreed to accept the same pay and allowances and to obey the rules and articles of war "now existing in the United States."

Johnny Reb had much to learn about the business of soldiering. Whether he was in the infantry, cavalry, or artillery, he first learned the bugle calls: Reveille, breakfast call, assembly, march, charge, retreat, dinner call, sick call, tattoo, and all the others; by these sounds he would live all his days as a soldier. Regardless of his outfit, he learned to march—to keep step, to stay in line, to column right or column left, to do an about face without tilting his torso as much as one degree from the perpendicular. Although he had grown up with shotgun and rifle, he must now learn how to carry his "piece," how to load and aim and fire it—instructions which he promptly forgot during his first engagement with the enemy. He must learn how to salute his officers and the language with which to address them, things which sometimes galled his soul if he did not respect an officer as a man or as a soldier. Not infrequently, even though he might not be an officer, he acquired an infantry textbook, Winfield Scott's *Infantry-Tactics* or William J. Hardee's *Rifle and Light Infantry Tactics,* which he read assiduously for a few days and then tossed aside. After all, the officers always told him what to do anyway; let them do the studying.

If Louisiana's Johnny Reb was a cavalry trooper rather than an infantryman, the business of soldiering was even more complicated. The bugle calls now included boots and saddles, to horse, walk, trot, gallop, column of fours right or column of fours left, draw sabers, and many others. He must engage in pistol practice—draw, ready, aim, fire—and he must acquire the fundamentals of saber positions and strokes—moulinet, point, cut, parry. He must learn the positions of the standard and the guidon in order that he might follow them in battle. He must learn that troopers shouted and yelled when charging infantry, but remained silent when charging other cavalry. He must learn to care for his horse properly, even though he had left his own farm or plantation horses but a few days ago. He must even learn how to get on his horse.

The soldier's training period was routine and monotonous, filled with small hardships and duties to which he as a civilian had been unaccustomed. Witness the account of one very young Louisiana soldier:

We get up at five o'clock to attend roll-call; at 6:30 get our coffee and our breakfast, which consists of crackers and salt pork; at 7:30, back to our tents and pack our knapsack, rub our guns, and get ready for parade at nine o'clock. We are now drilling at light infantry tactics (Hardee's), which occupies us until eleven. We then *wash our clothes, bring wood for the cook, also water* and various other things; dine at two, and again drill at four until dark; get our supper at seven; lie around until roll-call at nine; afterward go to bed to dream of home.

Before leaving for the front, most companies received battle flags from the admiring women of their communities. At the flag-presentation ceremony of the De Soto Rifles in late April, 1861, Miss Idelea Collens presented the colors and said: "Receive then, from your mothers and sisters, from those whose affections greet you, these colors woven by our feeble but reliant hands; and when this bright flag shall float before you on the battlefield, let it not only inspire you with the brave and patriotic ambition of a soldier aspiring to his own and his country's honor and glory, but also may it be a sign that cherished ones appeal to you to save them from a fanatical and heartless foe."

The color-sergeant, who received the flag, made a brief but impressive response: "Ladies, with high-beating hearts and pulses throbbing with emotion, we receive from your hands this beautiful flag, the proud emblem of our young republic. . . . May the God of battles look down upon us as we register a soldier's vow that no stain shall ever be found upon thy sacred folds, save the blood of those who attack thee or those who fall in thy defence. . . ."

So Louisiana's Johnny Reb became a soldier. But he never became really accustomed to soldiering, nor did he ever acquire a real liking for it. It was a duty to be performed, and for the most part he performed it to the best of his ability.

Problems Civil and Military. As the months of 1861 passed, civil and military problems emerged, some to remain unsolved throughout the war years. Governor Moore did the best that could have been done under the circumstances. Within the state his efforts were adequately rewarding; in his relations with other states and

31

with the Confederate government, however, little was accomplished in behalf of Louisiana. He constantly pleaded with President Davis for men and arms to reinforce the defenses of New Orleans and early in 1862 begged "in God's name, in the name of my State," that guns and ammunition be sent to Louisiana immediately. New Orleans fell a short time later.

Direct economic relief to soldiers' families was of governmental concern, but while there was considerable assistance from state, parish, and town governments throughout the war, most of the needed food, clothing, blankets, and medicinal supplies came from private sources. State-wide committees, associations, and societies of all types were organized, including "The Society of Ladies in Aid of the Confederate Army," "Aid to Volunteers' Families Committee," "Free Gift Lottery Association," "Ladies Volunteer Aid Association," and the "Association for the Relief of the Sick and Wounded Soldiers of Louisiana." Sewing and knitting "circles," volunteer relief groups, and nursing committees were organized in most communities. Many of these organizations continued their work throughout the war and for some time after its conclusion.

But in spite of the enthusiastic support of the war effort, speculators, slackers, and other disloyalists were at work. Smuggling and the selling of cotton to the enemy became so flagrant that in October, Governor Moore stopped all export shipments until the blockade should be lifted. A short time later he ordered that New Orleans and the surrounding parishes be searched for traitors and that they be arrested and their houses burned. Charges of "abolitionism" were not infrequent, and those found guilty of supporting such heresy were sent to jail for six months. William H. Russell reported that "the moral suasion of the lasso, of tarring and feathering, head-shaving, ducking, and horseponds, deportation on rails, and similar ethical processes are highly in favour." The New Orleans press became facetious at times over these methods of securing Confederate loyalty and lauded "the course of instruction in the humane institution for the amelioration of the condition of northern barbarians and abolition fanatics."

Measures for State Defense. During the early weeks of the Confederacy, Governor Moore became fearful of an attack upon New Orleans and the southern coast of the state. He appealed to the Confederate government to strengthen the forts below New Orleans and to stop the drain from the state of troops and supplies. But even Judah P. Benjamin, along with other Confederate officials, believed that the fears of Louisianians were "without cause" and that the defenses of New Orleans were adequate. In middle August, and again in September, 1861, General David E. Twiggs, the commanding general at New Orleans, appealed for reinforcements and munitions, but Confederate government officials, completely absorbed with the war in the East, gave little thought to the importance of the Crescent City nor to the problems of its defense.

Governor Moore's pleas to President Davis that New Orleans and the southern Louisiana coast "be no longer neglected" were supported by former Governor A. B. Roman, who flatly said: "A grave responsibility must rest on those who have not prevented such a state of things."

Lincoln had proclaimed a blockade of the Southern ports in middle April, 1861. In June the sloops *Powhatan* and *Brooklyn* arrived at the mouth of the Mississippi, and by October half a dozen Federal ships were guarding the Head of Passes. The Confederate naval commander at New Orleans was Commodore George N. Hollins, who, after his arrival the last of July, converted several river steamers into "warships." In October, Hollins decided "to lay a lance in rest," and on the night of the eleventh, with the iron ram *Manassas* leading, attacked the Federal blockading flotilla. After a short, blundering naval "battle" in which not a single man was even injured, the Confederate fleet steamed back up the river and the Federal fleet retired from the Head of Passes. Of this engagement a Federal officer later wrote: "I truly feel ashamed for our side, the idea of such ships as ours being driven down the river by nine guns."

By fall, seventy-one-year-old General Twiggs, who had been in poor health for some months, was confined to a wheel chair. On October 18, Major General Mansfield Lovell, a District of Columbia–born, West Point–trained, thirty-nine-year-old retired army officer living in New York City when the war began, became Commander of the Department of Louisiana, and the same day protested to the Confederate government that the city "first in importance in the Confederacy" had been drained "of arms, ammunition, medical stores, clothing and supplies for other points." In early December he reported that Forts Jackson and St. Philip had been reinforced, that the fortifications in the vicinity of New Orleans were manned by some 8,000 troops, and that 6,000 volunteers were in the city itself. The general, though not satisfied with the adequacy of the New Orleans defenses, believed that the city was "in a condition to resist an attack."

In his message to the Legislature in November, the Governor stressed the financial problems of the state, revealed that because of the blockade and the loss of Northern trade only one third of the 1860 taxes had been paid, and explained the monetary and tax problems of the Confederate government. He recommended a revision of the militia law, legislation promoting farm relief, and legislative action on civil and military emergencies. He praised the contributions of private citizens, particularly the women, and emphasized that "the people are ready for any effort and every sacrifice in this, the holiest of causes." The West Baton Rouge *Sugar Planter* considered his message "one of the best tempered papers that ever issued from an Executive of the State. It will be perused with pride and admiration by every Louisianian."

V

1862—The Fall of New Orleans and the Occupation of Southeastern Louisiana

The Naval Expedition Against New Orleans. The strategic importance of New Orleans and the Lower Mississippi Valley was obvious to Federal leaders from the beginning of the war, and a naval expedition against the Crescent City was officially discussed in Washington as early as September, 1861. After a series of conferences, a general plan of operation was agreed upon and Flag Officer David G. Farragut was appointed to command the expedition, with Commander David D. Porter, his younger foster brother, as head of the mortar flotilla. Farragut was ordered to "destroy the armed barriers which these deluded people have raised up against the power of the United States . . . to take advantage of the panic" the capture of New Orleans would cause, and to then "push a strong force up the river to take all their defenses in the rear."

Farragut's fleet, a powerful flotilla consisting of 18 ships, 6 mortar steamers, and 19 mortar boats, mounting over 250 guns, rendezvoused at Ship Island in late February, 1862, arrived at the mouth of the Mississippi in early March, and within a month had crossed the bar. By the middle of April the fleet and the troop ships, carrying Major General Benjamin F. Butler and his army of 18,000 men, moved up the river to a point just below Forts Jackson and St. Philip.

During the preceding months General Mansfield Lovell had greatly strengthened the defenses of New Orleans. Obstructions were sunk and piles were driven at the mouths of the city's bayou approaches and earthworks and batteries were erected to protect them. Forts Pike, Macomb, and Livingston, as well as Jackson and St. Philip, were repaired and their guns put in serviceable condition. Batteries were erected above and below the city and nearly eight miles of entrenchments dug against the possibility of a land attack. Construction of the ironclads *Louisiana* and *Mississippi*, and of other ships, was pushed as rapidly as possible, although many laborers refused to work night shifts. Lovell had only about

3,000 troops garrisoned in or near the city and a small naval force patrolling the lower river.

Forts Jackson and St. Philip, built shortly after the War of 1812, were star-shaped masonary fortifications facing each other at a bend in the river about seventy-five miles below New Orleans. Their 147 guns were a hodgepodge including everything from six-pounders to ten-inch Columbiads, while their garrisons totaled about 1,500 men, some of whom were lack-luster scrapings from New Orleans. Fort Jackson was commanded by Colonel Edward Higgins and Fort St. Philip by Captain M. T. Squires, both under the over-all command of General J. K. Duncan.

Passage of the Forts. About 2:00 A.M. on April 24, after a mortar bombardment of six days, Farragut ordered all hands piped to quarters and dashed "with full head of steam on, right into the teeth of the rebel forts, and gun boats, and rams, and fire-rafts, and floating batteries and all infernal machines of torpedoes and de-structives." A Confederate wrote that "every gun opened in the Forts. The vessels poured broadside after broadside as they rushed past. . . . It was so bright . . . that we could see . . . every man in the rigging, every man at the guns in the Forts, dark against the red sulphurous light." General Butler thought the scene had "never been exceeded" and Farragut later reported that "it was as if the artillery of Heaven were playing on earth." Said the Confederate eyewitness: "It was the most superb sight I ever witnessed—so flashing, so bewildering, so magnificent, so brief."

The Confederate ships rushed into the melee of fire rafts and oncoming Federal vessels. The partially completed *Manassas* criss-crossed among the enemy ships ramming and firing until her armor was pierced and her engines set afire, when she charged into the riverbank, burning. The unfinished and immobile *Louisiana,* an-chored to the riverbank, became a roaring, steel-casemented fort. The *Hartford,* Farragut's flagship, although run aground and rammed by a burning fire raft, somehow got off, put out the fire, and continued upriver. The flaming piles of wood on the riverbanks burned out, and Farragut reported that "we had nothing to aim at but the flash of their guns; it was very difficult to distinguish friends from foes." One by one the outgunned, underarmored, and ill-manned Confederate boats went down or were driven ashore to finally burn out and explode with shattering repercussions.

The forts had been passed by dawn and the battle was over. But, although badly battered, Forts Jackson and St. Philip, and the brave *Louisiana,* still held.

The news that the Federal fleet had passed the forts reached New Orleans late that morning and within an hour the city was panic-stricken; "the fire-bells were rung twelve times to call out the guards." Men and women wandered aimlessly or ran about the streets, passing closed stores, schools, and public buildings. Civil and military officials ordered destroyed all supplies that might be of

35

value to the Federals, so warehouses containing over 15,000 bales of cotton and large stocks of tobacco and other products, coalyards, and lumberyards were set afire; factory machinery was smashed; dry docks were sunk; hogsheads of sugar and molasses and barrels of wines and liquors were dumped into the streets.

Although General Lovell had advised the naval officials either to move all ships and gunboats up the Mississippi or to attempt to run through the Federal blockade to Mobile, the vessels were fired and pushed away from the wharves to drift aimlessly down the river. These craft might have been used to advantage later in attempting to hold the Mississippi.

General Lovell had no alternative but to evacuate New Orleans, and as the troop trains pulled out they left defenseless a burning city filled with "the wildest confusion." The crowds continued to mill about all that day and many people thronged the streets throughout the night; by the morning of the twenty-fifth they had turned into a frightened, embittered mob, made even more angry by a blustering wind and driving rain. The flaming, unfinished hulk of the ironclad *Mississippi*, fired by her builders to prevent capture, floated past the city, causing one eyewitness to say that it impressed him "more strongly with an idea of warfare than all the fighting and slaughter I had ever seen." The newspapers had assured the people they were safe, and as Marion Southwood wrote, they all "felt how cruelly we had been deceived."

The mob began looting the city, while Home Guards and the Committee of Public Safety vainly attempted to restore order. Mayor John T. Monroe finally mobilized the foreign brigades, and they soon brought the central sections and the levee areas under control. About noon the Federal fleet passed the booming batteries at Chalmette and slowly rounded Slaughterhouse Point, "silent, grim, and terrible." Within two hours the "dusky, long, morose, demonlike Yankee steamers" were in front of New Orleans, riding high on the nine-foot river crest, high enough so that their guns could rake the streets. Thousands of citizens thronged the levee, while a woman waved the Confederate flag and a fifer shrilled "The Bonnie Blue Flag" and "Dixie" under the cannon of the flagship U.S.S. *Hartford*.

The Occupation of New Orleans. Shortly after the fleet anchored, Captain Theodorus Bailey and Lieutenant George Perkins came ashore, walked through the jeering, threatening mob to the City Hall, and presented Farragut's demand for the immediate surrender of New Orleans, the lowering of the Confederate flag from the City Hall and other buildings, and the raising of the United States flag over the post office, the customhouse, and the mint. The Mayor explained that General Lovell was still technically in command of the city, as it had been under martial law since the middle of March, but General Lovell pointed out that he was in the process of evacuating New Orleans and that the matter of surrender therefore was up to the city officials. The two Federal officers returned to the fleet after the Mayor had promised to confer with the City Council.

About ten o'clock the next morning the Mayor met with the Council, which approved a letter Pierre Soule had written for the Mayor to send to Farragut. While the letter tersely informed Farragut that "the city is yours by the power of brutal force" and that the officials would *not* lower the Confederate flags, the Council attached a resolution guaranteeing that no resistance would be made to the forces of the United States.

Before these communications could be sent to Farragut, two more Federal officers, Lieutenant Albert Kautz and Midshipman John H. Read, accompanied by about twenty marines, arrived at the landing. A lieutenant of the Crescent Reserves refused permission for the marines to land but escorted Kautz and Read to the Mayor's office. Again the Mayor refused Farragut's demands for surrender.

As these negotiations were progressing, an incident occurred which would have serious repercussions. A detachment of Federals landed and raised the United States flag over the mint, but a small group of citizens immediately pulled it down. One of the citizens was William B. Mumford, whom General Butler would hang for the act a little over a month later.

Sunday, the twenty-seventh, was comparatively calm and quiet, but on Monday the Mayor received from Farragut a short note in which the Flag Officer regretted that the Confederate and Louisiana flags had not been removed, protested the pulling down of the United States flag at the mint, threatened to fire upon the city, and demanded that the women and children be removed within two days. Monroe replied that it was impossible to evacuate the women and children on short notice and that "we will stand your bombardment, unarmed and undefended as we are."

On May 29, Farragut informed Monroe that he was "about to raise the flag of the United States." The Mayor issued a proclamation to the people, pleading that no "violence or disorder" occur and emphasizing that "the honor and dignity of New Orleans have been maintained." About noon, Captain Henry H. Bell landed a large detachment of marines and sailors, marched to the customhouse, raised the United States flag, and then moved down St. Charles Street to the City Hall at Lafayette Square. He went to the Mayor's office and asked him to order the lowering of the state flag. Monroe refused, and "in a few minutes Lieutenant Kautz went to the roof, cut the halyards with his sword," and Boatswain's Mate George Russell pulled the emblem down.

The city of New Orleans had not "surrendered" to the United States naval forces under Flag Officer Farragut; neither had it been "captured" through a military or naval attack. Although the technical meaning of the words may be argued, the fact remains that the city was simply "occupied."

The Federal troops, under the command of General Benjamin F. Butler, arrived about noon on May 1, landed at sundown, and took formal possession of the city.

Some authorities have argued that the fall of New Orleans directly resulted in the loss of the war. Certainly it meant the loss of southeastern Louisiana, the severing of the lower Mississippi River, and the cutting off of the Louisiana salt and Texas beef trade. It gave the Federal forces what would become the most important naval base in the South. It aided materially in the final cutting off of the entire Mississippi River at Vicksburg and Port Hudson, and it lost to the South its greatest industrial center. Most important of all, the city's fall did irreparable damage to the morale of Southern soldiers and civilians.

Why had the Crescent City fallen? The South simply did not have adequate quantities and types of military ordnance nor sufficient numbers of trained personnel at the point of contact with the invading forces to repel them. Regardless of the basic reasons for the loss of the city, General Lovell was the man held responsible and his military career was ruined. A year later, at his own request, he faced a court of inquiry and was cleared; but the court's decision was not promulgated until November, 1863. Despite the support of Joseph E. Johnston and Robert E. Lee, he was not given another military assignment until only two months before the end of the war.

State Governmental and Military Reorganization. Plans were made immediately after the fall of New Orleans to remove the state capital from Baton Rouge to Opelousas. The Governor ordered the destruction of cotton, sugar, tobacco, and other crops and supplies to prevent their falling into enemy hands. He wrote President Davis a pathetic letter saying that there was but one Confederate officer in the state, that Louisiana had "sent more than 30,000 men into the field," and that at least part of the state's misfortunes had been caused by a lack of trained military leadership. He began the organization of a state army, enlisted companies of Partisan Rangers, and established training camps in New Iberia, Opelousas, and Monroe.

Meanwhile, the Confederate territory west of the Mississippi had been designated as the Trans-Mississippi Department and in July, General T. H. Holmes was placed in command. The Governor wrote bitterly to the Secretary of War that when he had "begged for an officer" the Confederate government had answered by attaching Louisiana to a military department headquartered in Little Rock, Arkansas. His protests bore some fruit, for the following month General Richard Taylor was given command of the District of Western Louisiana. The Governor and the Legislature worked well with local officials and with Taylor in providing as much as possible for the civil and military needs of the state, although Taylor complained that the Confederate government provided no funds, no soldiers, and no arms and ammunition for Louisiana.

A portion of Farragut's fleet moved up the Mississippi immediately after the fall of New Orleans, indiscriminately tossing shells into towns and at plantation homes, although, as one Northern historian has remarked, it met "no resistance more serious than the wordy protests of mayors of undefended cities." Baton Rouge was shelled and then occupied by some 1,500 troops under the command of General Thomas Williams. Soon heavy ironclads and smaller, lighter armed vessels called "tinclads" were patrolling the lower sections of the Mississippi.

During this period southeast Louisianians were initiated into the deliberate and wanton destruction and looting of private property, a Federal practice which continued during the entire war and through which Louisiana suffered more financial loss than did any other Southern state. General Thomas Williams once reported that the Wisconsin and Michigan regiments "regard pillaging not only right in itself but a soldierly accomplishment." Donaldsonville was burned on August 9 in reprisal for snipers having fired upon Federal ships from the vicinity of the town. The bombardment of sugarhouses became something of a Federal naval sport during the summer and fall months of 1862, and in November young Robert Patrick reported in his diary that the gunboats "were firing on some sugar houses on the other side of the river this morning which they are very good at considering the houses cannot fire back, and is a very safe way of carrying on a war."

Raiders in the New Orleans–Donaldsonville–Brashear City Triangle. The Mississippi River turns almost straight eastward at Donaldsonville, while Bayou Lafourche, one of its old deltas, angles off to the southeast. Up the Atchafalaya, a little more than a score of miles from its mouth, was Brashear City, present-day Morgan City, which was connected with Algiers, on the west side of the Mississippi opposite New Orleans, by the New Orleans, Opelousas, and Great Western Railroad. The line was the important connecting link with the Teche Country, which in turn was the southern gateway to Central Louisiana. During the summer of 1862 the rich agricultural triangle formed by New Orleans, Donaldsonville, and Brashear City was the scene of considerable raiding by small bodies of Federal troops temporarily operating from Jefferson Station, Bayou des Allemands, Lafourche Crossing, Bayou Boeuf, and other stations along the railroad.

On May 5, Butler sent Colonel James W. McMillan with a small detachment on a raiding expedition all along the railroad to Brashear City, during which they captured several cannon and a quantity of supplies. Late in the month Confederate Captain E. W. Fuller of the St. Martin Rangers captured a train at Bayou Boeuf, moved eastward to Jefferson Station, about nine miles from Algiers, removed several rails from the track, cut the levee, and returned to Brashear City, picking up railroad rolling stock along the way and burning the bridges at Des Allemands, Raceland, and Bayou Boeuf.

Shortly afterward, three companies of the Eighth Vermont Volunteers made "an unopposed excursion to Thibodaux," where they destroyed a foundry, serenaded the young ladies of the seminary, gave three cheers for the Stars and Stripes, and then marched away, their band playing "Yankee Doodle." In June, Governor Moore sent Captain James A. McWaters and Captain S. D. Ashe with companies of Partisan Rangers to the area to stop trade with New Orleans and to suppress the activities of the Unionists. By the end of the year Des Allemands was the westernmost Federal outpost on the railroad.

In September, General Richard Taylor protested to General Butler of the behavior of the "ruthless soldiery," who were carrying off or destroying "every movable object" on the plantations of this section and who were indecently searching women and children and taking wearing apparel and jewelry from their persons. He finally threatened, upon the repetition of these acts of "lawless violence," to begin the execution of prisoners of war.

The Battle of Baton Rouge. The Federals had occupied Baton Rouge on May 8 and had then moved up the river to secure Vicksburg, but the attack failed and General Thomas Williams returned to Baton Rouge. When it became obvious that Vicksburg was at least temporarily safe, Confederate General John C. Breckenridge was sent southward from Vicksburg with a small force to recapture Baton Rouge. At the same time the little Confederate river fleet, led by the ironclad *Arkansas*, moved down-river to co-operate with Breckenridge.

Breckenridge proceeded by rail to Camp Moore and then moved his army to Greenwell Springs, where he learned that the *Arkansas* had already passed Bayou Sara. He rapidly marched to Baton Rouge, arriving there a little after midnight on the morning of August 5, and bivouacked east of Magnolia Cemetery.

The Confederates moved out along the Greenwell Springs Road at dawn, driving the Federal pickets before them. The Federal troops were concentrated along present-day Nineteenth Street from Government Street to North Street. The Confederate left wing, after very hard fighting, advanced to within about a mile of the river; the right wing, meanwhile, moved down Plank Road to its juncture with the Bayou Sara Road, and then to a point just north of the Cemetery, where the heaviest fighting of the day occurred. The Federals were slowly pushed back toward the United States Military Barracks, the central portion of the town, and the State House, and the firing gradually ceased as they gained the shelter of their supporting river fleet. The battle had lasted about six hours.

The Confederates held their positions, waiting for the arrival of the *Arkansas*. About four o'clock in the afternoon Breckenridge received the report that her machinery had failed about four miles north of the city and there was little hope that she could be brought into action.* Realizing that he could not take Baton Rouge without heavy artillery support, Breckenridge ordered his army to withdraw toward the Comite River.

A few days later Breckenridge moved to Port Hudson and began construction of heavy batteries. After having burned a number of buildings, the Federals evacuated Baton Rouge on August 21, thus giving the Confederates control of the Mississippi River northward to Vicksburg. Butler ordered the city destroyed, but at the last moment countermanded the order. A Federal officer wrote, however, that "this place has been nearly completely sacked by the soldiery. . . . Even officers' tents are filled with furniture from deserted houses."

General Weitzel's Campaign Along Bayou Lafourche. In middle August, Major John L. Lewis was ordered to Thibodaux, where he was joined a short time later by a Texas Cavalry battalion. By the beginning of fall, Brigadier General Alfred Mouton had nearly 1,500 men and two batteries of artillery under his command in the vicinity of Napoleonville, and his forces soon captured Des Allemands, ambushed a train at Boutte Station, and pushed the Federal outposts back to within a few miles of Algiers. General Taylor wrote that these "trifling" successes, "the first in the State since the loss of New Orleans," immeasurably improved citizen morale throughout the state.

Late the next month, General Godfrey Weitzel with a Federal force of about 4,000 men began to move down Bayou Lafourche, General Mouton slowly retreating ahead of him. At Labadieville, on October 27, Colonel Leopold Armant, with about 1,000 troops, including the Eighteenth Louisiana Infantry, the old "Dix-huitième," attempted to halt the advance of about twice that number of the enemy, but failed. The Federals, however, because of their severe losses, were not able to follow up their victory.

General Mouton continued slowly down the bayou to Thibodaux and then westward to Brashear City. A strong flotilla of Federal gunboats arrived at Berwick Bay shortly after Mouton had crossed the Atchafalaya. The Confederates moved up the Teche about a dozen miles from Brashear City to Bisland, where they threw up a light earthwork extending from the Teche northward to Grand Lake and southward to the uncompleted New Orleans, Opelousas, and Great Western Railroad, which ran along the edge of the Gulf

* The *Arkansas*, upon the arrival of the Federal river fleet, was set afire and burned by her crew.

marshes. Weitzel slowly followed Mouton, occupied Brashear City, and at the year's end was making sniping attacks upon the Confederates.

The End of the Year. In November, Major General Nathaniel P. Banks sailed from New York for New Orleans with a force of about 20,000 men. His orders were to relieve General Butler of his command of the Department of the Gulf, recapture Baton Rouge, take Port Hudson, send an expedition into Texas, occupy the Red River as a basis of future operations against Texas and Arkansas, and co-operate with General U. S. Grant in his campaign against Vicksburg. He arrived at New Orleans the middle of December. Banks had a total of nearly 40,000 men in his department, most of them in Louisiana, while Taylor opposed him with considerably less than one fourth that number, concentrated for the most part between Alexandria and Brashear City.

Banks immediately sent General Cuvier Grover with a force of 10,000 men up the Mississippi River to occupy Baton Rouge, which he called "the first rebel position on the river." The small Confederate force was driven off without difficulty and Baton Rouge was occupied on December 17. Negro troops quartered in the capitol purportedly set it afire by accident on the evening of the twenty-eighth. The loss was not serious, but early the next morning another fire was discovered, and this time the interior of the building was completely burned out. The books which had remained in the State Library after the looting of the previous summer and many state and local archives were completely destroyed.

The year 1862 had been a fateful and tragic one for the Pelican State. New Orleans had been occupied by Federal forces; Baton Rouge had been twice captured and the capitol had been burned. Sections of southeastern and southern Louisiana had been ravaged and sacked by invading troops, as had been parts of the northeastern section of the state. Federal gunboats were in complete possession of the lower Mississippi.

VI

1863—The Campaigns Along the Mississippi and the Teche

The Invasion of Northeast Louisiana. In early February, 1863, General E. Kirby Smith was placed in command of the Confederate Trans-Mississippi Department and a month later arrived at Alexandria. Permanently headquartered in Shreveport, by the middle of the year he had extended his military and civil activities to the point that he was sending diplomatic agents to Mexico, appointing civil officials and army officers, making military promotions, controlling cotton exports, and even handling certain problems of Confederate conscription. His critics began to call the department "Kirby-Smithdom."

While Governor Moore and General Richard Taylor had done their best to supply matériel and military personnel for the protection of the state, Taylor reported early in the year that he had only about 4,000 men properly equipped and fit for duty. The inadequacy of Confederate defensive forces in the state, and the Union possession of large supply bases at New Orleans and Memphis put the Federals in position to begin military operations along the Mississippi.

The opening of the Mississippi through the capture of Vicksburg and Port Hudson was a paramount Federal military objective in 1863. Two attempts to capture Vicksburg in 1862 had failed; so late that year the Federals decided to cross the Mississippi into Arkansas, move down the west side of the river into Louisiana to some point south of Vicksburg, recross the river, and then proceed against the Confederate stronghold from the rear.

General U. S. Grant moved into northeast Louisiana in December, 1862, and landed a division of troops under General A. J. Smith at Milliken's Bend, about twenty miles above Vicksburg, on Christmas Day. Lake Providence and Carroll Parish were quickly occupied, and the Federal forces began to move down the river. A canal to enable the Federal river fleet to bypass the city was started at a narrow point on a long bend of the river about five miles south of Vicksburg.

Dredge boats were brought down from Memphis, and from January, 1863, work on the sixty-foot-wide and nine-foot-deep canal proceeded rapidly. It was practically completed by early March, but heavy rains flooded the entire area, driving troops and canal laborers away from the project. A Federal soldier reported that "Our canal here don't amount to much. It is full of water, but manifests no disposition to change the channel of the Mississippi. It is a very small affair, and we can hardly work a barge through it for stumps." Shortly thereafter the scheme was abandoned.* Other plans of even greater magnitude to bypass Vicksburg were soon conceived, but by the middle of March all waterways-connecting projects had been given up.

Meanwhile, the area from the Arkansas line to St. Joseph had been overrun by Federal troops, who had wrought general, needless destruction of property along their entire path. Clifton Parkhurst, who was with the Sixteenth Iowa Infantry, wrote graphicly: "We marched for fifteen miles along Lake St. Joseph. . . . and around its fertile shores had been one of the garden spots of Louisiana. . . . Only the day before, expensive homes, sugar mills, and cotton plantations of great cost looked out upon the placid lake in proud serenity. Now, where we marched, were smouldering ruins, and for miles ahead we could see smoke and flames wrapping roofs and walls that towered high."

Grant began crossing the Mississippi a few miles north of St. Joseph on April 30 and the next day moved his army eastward to Port Gibson, Mississippi. A little over two weeks later, he began the siege of Vicksburg.

Banks's Bayou Teche Campaign. In late January, General Banks ordered General Godfrey Weitzel to move to Brashear City and then to advance up the Teche; at the same time he ordered General W. H. Emory to march westward from Plaquemine to join Weitzel for an attack upon Butte-a-la-Rose, a Confederate fortified position on the Atchafalaya River east of present-day Lafayette. The joint expedition failed when Emory was unable to cross the swampy country west of Plaquemine and could not navigate Bayou Plaquemine because it contained an unusual amount of accumulated driftwood.

In early April, Banks ordered Generals Cuvier Grover and W. H. Emory to move from Baton Rouge to Donaldsonville, thence down the Lafourche and across to Brashear City, to join forces with General Godfrey Weitzel for an invasion of the Teche Country. Banks arrived from New Orleans on April 8 to take personal command of the unified force of about 17,000 men, which was opposed by General Richard Taylor and a weak Confederate army mustering only some 5,000 effectives.

* In 1876 the Mississippi River cut through this peninsula, a short distance above the projected canal, finally isolating Vicksburg. Traces of "Grant's Canal" may still be seen.

Banks began his movement up the Teche on April 11, and two days later drove the Confederates back at Pattersonville. Fort Bisland, flanked by General Grover, who moved up Grand Lake in transports, had to be abandoned, but not before "the Yankees," according to Texas soldier Theophilus Noel, "had danced to our music."

The Battle of Franklin was a bitterly fought engagement, marked by Confederate infantry and cavalry counterattacks along the bayou road for some distance below and above the town. In one of the most brilliant holding actions of the entire war, Taylor held on until his artillery and wagon train reached New Iberia.

The Confederates retreated slowly and deliberately through New Iberia and Vermilionville, fought a sharp, defensive engagement at Bayou Vermilion, then moved northward toward Opelousas. Noel reported that "at Opelousas we had a breathing spell. Here we overtook our baggage and commissary train, and the enemy not pushing us with his usual ferocity, we were allowed to cook once more for ourselves." For some days the Confederates had been constantly on the move, "scarcely a moment passed by that guns could not be heard, and scarcely an hour but what the enemy's artillery was engaged."

Taylor moved his troops northward from Opelousas, which Banks occupied on April 20, to the valley of the Red River. The Federals remained in defensive positions at Opelousas for about two weeks, apparently fearing an attack by General Alfred Mouton, in striking distance to the westward. Admiral David Porter then moved the Federal flotilla up the Red River and docked at Alexandria on May 7, a few hours before Banks arrived. A week later Banks moved down the Red River and on May 23 crossed the Mississippi at Bayou Sara.

The campaign had little military significance, for Banks's only objectives were to keep the Confederate troops in the area occupied and to destroy "the materials upon which an army could be organized or supported in that country." The Federal general reported that he had captured over 2,500 prisoners and more than 20 cannon; Taylor later wrote in reply that since his entire fighting force had numbered but few more than 2,500, it was "rather startling to learn that we were all captured." Historian Fred H. Harrington wrote that Banks "grabbed three million dollars' worth of spoils— ten thousand bales of cotton, much sugar and molasses, ten thousand head of cattle and nearly as many mules and horses. These were public seizures; despite punishment of looters, there were individual acquisitions, too. 'Boys are getting fat,' commented one observer, while others noted that Union soldiers had taken watches, dishes, earrings, Bibles, portraits, women's clothing."

Berwick City was the entrepôt for all "confiscated" goods south of Opelousas, and Federal Colonel A. J. H. Duganne wrote that "Contrabands and cotton bales are hurried off upon railway-flats.

Shrewd cattlebrokers, after swarming about the quartermaster's doors, drive off their bargains of beeves. Mules are trotted away. . . . Carts, chaises, family coaches, saddles, harnesses, debris of Attakapas 'confiscation,' are invoiced, via rail, to New Orleans auction blocks." Then Berwick City "caught" fire, and for a day and a night "roofs, corridors, galleries, are ignited, and the red element extends and mounts, right and left, in lurid wings," until "the fire becomes exhausted, for lack of materials to feed upon." The Teche Country had been left a gutted, blackened waste. In General Banks's opinion, his movement from Brashear City to Alexandria had been "the cleanest . . . . best conceived and best executed campaign of the war."

The Siege of Port Hudson. The Confederates had selected the Port Hudson area as the site for a major river stronghold in August, 1862, after the Battle of Baton Rouge, and General W. N. R. Beall was placed in charge of building the fortifications. He constructed a remarkably strong series of earthworks; beginning at Ross's Landing, about a mile below Port Hudson, the lines ran northeasterly through broken, timbered ground cut by deep ravines, then northward across a series of fields and pastures broken only by scattered clumps of trees (one of them called, prophetically, "Slaughter's Field"), then northwest and west through extremely rough, ravine-cut timberland to the Mississippi River swamps at the mouth of Thompson's Creek. The parapets averaged about twenty feet in thickness, and in front of them were ditches twelve to fifteen feet deep. Along the eighty-foot bluff at Port Hudson were twenty heavy cannon, while supporting the four miles of land-defense lines were several batteries of artillery totaling about thirty pieces.

General Franklin Gardner, who had succeeded General Beall the last of December, 1862, commanded Port Hudson's garrison of between 6,500 and 7,000 men. General Banks's Federal besieging forces varied between 30,000 and 40,000 men. In addition, he had sufficient artillery of all calibers, unlimited amounts of ammunition, a constant flow of supplies through the depots at Baton Rouge, and an excellent cavalry force to guard his rear.

Banks ordered a frontal assault on May 27, before all of his army had arrived and before his own officers could even make a good reconnaissance. He attacked the Confederate left, then ordered several charges on the extreme right, but the unco-ordinated Federal attacks failed all along the Confederate lines. The fiasco cost the Union general nearly 2,000 casualties.

A second grand assault was made on June 14, but the Federal feint upon the Confederate right wing at a point called the "Citadel" somehow miscarried, and the main thrust upon the left completely failed. Banks now settled down to regular siege operations, for, according to one Federal soldier, the rank and file had given notice that they would make no more grand assaults in close order across long distances of open terrain. One Federal officer wrote that "a pair of Turkish pashas would have been quite as enterprising and inventive" as Banks and Gardner. Another refused to lead his men in a hopeless charge, saying to his aide: "Now go back to General Grover. Tell him that I have formed the column, and that, if he wants it to charge, he may come and lead it. I for my part am not going to take it into that slaughter pen."

The siege continued. One Federal wrote that "every morning I was awakened by the popping of rifles and the whistling of balls; hardly a day passed that I did not hear the loud exclamations of the wounded, or see corpses borne to the rear; and the gamut of my good-night lullaby varied all the way from Minie rifles to sixty-eight pounders." A Confederate wrote that "no one can 'get used' to a bombardment. . . . It has the tendency to make a man either a good Christian or a fatalist." Another Federal wrote that the battleground in front of the Confederate lines looked "as if a tornado had swept across . . . a fiery storm [such] as fell upon Sodom and Gomorrah. . . . The surface of the earth was ploughed and seared; the sand-bags on the breastwork, that I have looked at so often from our cover, were pierced and powder-stained; and, in the old rifle-pits, bloody sacking told where there had been killed and wounded men." The booming cannon could be heard in Baton Rouge, twenty miles down the river, and even in Woodville, Mississippi, thirty-five miles to the north.

The day-by-day fighting was much the same. The Confederates lay behind their breastworks and in their trenches and rifle pits; the Federals, particularly on the left and right wings where the terrain was timbered and rough, dug and tunneled and wormed as close to the Confederate lines as possible. The opponents called out to each other, "Why don't you come over?" or "Why don't you come out and fight us?" Confederates yelled the words they had cut on trees along the road approaches to Port Hudson, "Beware, Yankee! This is a hard road to travel." When long-fused grenades were tossed within the lines, the Confederates caught them with blankets and tossed them back. Closely dug-in enemies became acquainted, and fraternization between lines began, and tobacco, coffee, and newspapers were exchanged for sugar and molasses. When officers appeared, the men sounded off with "Look out, Yank, we're going to fire" or "Get under cover now, Johnnie."

While the Federal cannonading continued, General Richard Taylor failed in his attempt to send supplies across the Mississippi to the besieged fort. General Gardner realized that assistance from other Confederate forces was impossible, but stubbornly held on. The last quarter-ration of beef was distributed on June 29. Two days later a wounded mule was butchered and the meat served at an officers' mess. It was pronounced an excellent dish: "The flesh of mules is of a darker color than beef, of a finer grain, quite tender and juicy, and has a flavor something between that of beef and

47

venison." Thereafter mule and horse meat became much in demand, although horse meat was "not equal to mule." Rats were pronounced "quite a luxury—superior, in the opinion of those who eat them, to spring chicken." Fish stunned by exploding shells in the Mississippi were collected and sold at from $5.00 to $50.00 each, depending upon their size. Medicines at last gave out, and chills and fevers and even more serious disorders became rampant within the fort.

On July 7, Banks received the news of the surrender of Vicksburg and immediately communicated the information to the Confederates. On the eighth, a board of officers worked out the terms of the surrender of Port Hudson, and General Gardner issued General Order No. 61, congratulating his men: "The cheerfulness, bravery and zeal displayed by the troops during the hardships and suffering of this long siege has never been surpassed, and every man can feel the proud satisfaction that he has done his part in the heroic defense of Port Hudson."

The battered fort had withstood over sixty days of bombardment by the Federal river fleet and forty-five days of actual siege. Its defenders had beaten back two grand, frontal assaults and a score of attempts to storm individual salients of the earthworks. Both Confederate and Federal losses had been heavy, the Fifteenth Arkansas, for example, losing 132 killed and wounded out of 392 officers and men in the May 27 defense of "Fort Desperate." The defenders were proud of their heroic stand; their enemies complimented them upon "the skill and bravery" of their defense.

The Confederate troops paraded at 6:00 A.M. on July 9, "in line of battle, in the same order they are now at the breastworks." Gardner rode along the lines amidst the cheers of his men "whose affection and confidence he had permanently gained during the days and weeks of trial." The Federal column approached, led by General George L. Andrews. Gardner advanced with drawn sword and presented it to Andrews, who refused it, saying, "I return your sword as a proper compliment to the gallant commander of such gallant troops—conduct that would be heroic in another cause." And Gardner replied, slamming the sword back into its scabbard, "This is neither the time nor place to discuss the cause."

The Confederate soldiers grounded arms and the Federal troops took their positions. The American flag was raised, a salute was fired, and the ceremony was over. The Mississippi River was now open to the sea. But, as historian Jefferson Davis Bragg has written: "One marvels now that Appomattox was still twenty-two months away."

Taylor's Campaign Against New Orleans. After Banks began his besieging of Port Hudson, General E. Kirby Smith, Commander of the Trans-Mississippi Department, ordered General Richard Taylor to move into northeastern Louisiana to attack Grant's occupying troops. Taylor protested that the cutting of Grant's lines of communication and supply from St. Joseph to Lake Providence would in no way force him to give up the investment of Vicksburg, and that the best way to aid the Mississippi citadel was "to capture the Berwick Bay fortifications, overrun the Lafourche, interrupt Banks's communications with New Orleans, and threaten the city itself." But Smith was adamant.

In early June, Taylor moved against New Carthage, via New River and the Tensas, captured Richmond, and drove the small bodies of scattered Federal occupying troops to the protection of their river gunboats at Young's Point, Duckport, Milliken's Bend, Goodrich's Landing, and Lake Providence. The fighting in these comparatively small engagements was particularly fierce, due perhaps to the large numbers of Louisiana-enlisted Federal Negro troops. A modern historian has written that at Milliken's Bend "the Negro troops on the line of resistance" broke at the first fire; a contemporary Confederate battle report, however, stated that the "charge was resisted by the negro portion of the enemy's force with considerable obstinacy, while the white or true Yankee portion ran like whipped curs almost as soon as the charge was ordered." The Federals, however, held their river depots and could not be dislodged. Taylor was then ordered back to the Red River to attack the Federals at Port Hudson or to move against New Orleans; General John G. Walker, with some 4,500 men, remained in northeast Louisiana to harass the enemy, threaten Grant's supply lines, and perhaps assist in carrying out Kirby Smith's visionary plan to relieve Vicksburg by occupying Helena, Arkansas.

Taylor assembled an army of about 3,000 men at Alexandria. One detachment under Colonel J. P. Major moved from Opelousas to Plaquemine to Thibodaux, and then westward along the railroad toward Brashear City. Another body of troops, under Generals Alfred Mouton and Thomas Green, moved down the Teche. The two Confederate armies attacked the Federal forces at Brashear City on the night of June 22 and captured the town at dawn the following morning. Taylor reported laconically: "I push on to La Fourche this evening."

Taylor sent one detachment under General Green to attack Donaldsonville, while Mouton moved eastward, occupied Lafourche Crossing, and posted his pickets within twenty miles of New Orleans. Green attacked the Donaldsonville earthworks about 1:30 A.M. on the morning of June 28. The fighting continued until daylight, when the Confederates pulled back their forces and moved down the Mississippi a few miles, to erect batteries commanding the river. General W. H. Emory, the Federal commander at New Orleans, begged Banks for immediate assistance, but Banks replied that Port Hudson and Vicksburg were the paramount Federal objectives, and that he was confident both would be forced to capitulate shortly.

Vicksburg surrendered on July 4, Port Hudson five days later, and that same afternoon Banks moved troops down the river to Donaldsonville. An indecisive battle was fought at Lafourche Crossing on July 13, and shortly afterwards Taylor withdrew all his forces to Brashear City. He leisurely collected his captured guns, munitions, and supplies and moved up the Teche. Although the Federals occupied Brashear City on July 22, they made no attempt to pursue the Confederates. Taylor always insisted that had his command been reinforced with Walker's northeast Louisiana forces, he could have recaptured New Orleans and thus have forced major changes in Federal operations along the Mississippi.

During the fall months Taylor played cat and mouse with the Federals in South Louisiana. In early October, Federal General William B. Franklin advanced up the Teche toward Opelousas. Taylor fought sharp delaying actions at New Iberia, Vermilionville, Carrion Crow, Rodgers' Plantation, Hudson's Plantation, and Grand Coteau, finally halting the Federal advance at Bayou Courtableau, just east of Opelousas, in early November. By December the Federals were back at Brashear City and General Kirby Smith had written Richmond that Taylor was "cautious, yet bold; always prepared for and anticipating the enemy; concentrating skillfully upon his main force, holding it in check, and crippling its movements; promptly striking his detached columns, routing and destroying them." At the year's end Taylor was headquartered at Opelousas, his army scattered along the Teche.

River and Bayou Warfare. At the beginning of the war, both nations began building vessels for operation on the rivers and bayous of the South. Both converted river steamers to military use and built ironclads, rams, gunboats, tinclads, monitors, and other types of craft, but the industrial North, aided materially by the inventive genius of engineer James B. Eads, far outbuilt the South.

Control of the Mississippi River was the keystone to the over-all strategy of the war in the West. The South controlled the river at the war's beginning and vainly attempted to retain possession. The North's strategy proposed an offensive war to sweep it free of Confederate vessels and to provide mobile siege weapons, river-craft protection, artillery support for ground operations, and supply for military campaigns and individual armies.

After the fall of New Orleans, Farragut and Porter attempted to gain control of the entire Mississippi, but ran into stumbling blocks at Port Hudson and Vicksburg. Federal vessels began running past Vicksburg in early February, 1863, when the ram *Queen of the West* ran "the gauntlet in broad daylight," being under fire from the shore batteries for nearly an hour. The *Queen* had orders to destroy the Confederate steamer *Vicksburg,* and Admiral Porter wrote to Colonel Charles R. Ellet, the *Queen's* commander, that "It will not be part of your duty to save the lives of those on board [the *Vicksburg*]." Ellet rammed the Confederate steamer but did little damage and was soon driven off. After capturing several Confederate steamers south of Vicksburg, the *Queen* engaged shore batteries on the lower Red River on February 14, ran aground, and was captured.

The Federal gunboat *Indianola* followed the *Queen* to the mouth of the Red River, then moved back up the Mississippi. A small Confederate river fleet of four vessels, led by the armed ram *Webb,* a converted side-wheel steamer, followed and attacked the heavier-armed *Indianola* on the night of February 24. After being rammed half a dozen times, the *Indianola* heaved her guns overboard and ran ashore, where her crew surrendered. The Confederates once more controlled the Mississippi from Vicksburg to Port Hudson.

On the night of March 14, Farragut led a small fleet up the Mississippi in the hope of running past the Port Hudson river batteries. The *Richmond* and the *Genesee* were badly pounded and drifted downstream, and shortly were followed by the *Monongahela* and the *Kineo.* The *Mississippi*'s pilot, confused by the fog and flashing guns, ran his craft into the west bank opposite the Confederate batteries. She was finally worked loose from the bank and then drifted down the river, as a Federal soldier wrote, "abandoned, beaten with shot, ragged through her whole frame where shells had torn and burst . . . a freight of dead men were on her deck, and the bodies of drowned men floated about her hoary hull." But Farragut's flagship, the *Hartford,* and the *Albatross,* got through, greatly altering the strategic position of the Federal forces, for the Red River mouth and the western shores of the Mississippi could now be blockaded, sealing off supplies destined for Vicksburg and Port Hudson.

After the fall of Port Hudson the Federals held the entire length of the Mississippi, while the Confederates had only one sizable vessel in the entire state, the *Webb,* operating on the Red River above Alexandria. Federal control of the Mississippi was of major importance to the war in the West, and the control of the smaller streams and bayous of Louisiana by Federal vessels seriously affected the operations of Confederate armies in Louisiana.

VII

1864—The Red River Campaign

Military Situation at the Beginning of the Year. Louisiana was in a perilous military position at the beginning of 1864. Poised in Arkansas was a Federal force of about 25,000, opposed by a weakened Confederate army of some 7,000. General W. T. Sherman commanded forces totaling over 100,000 in Mississippi, in opposition to Confederate armies of less than half that number. General Banks had about 60,000 men in the southeastern Louisiana parishes and New Orleans, against which Kirby Smith could muster less than 20,000. The Federals were concentrated in the vicinity of Baton Rouge, Port Hudson, and Berwick City, while the Confederates were scattered along the lower Red River and Bayou Teche. While the Federals were in a position to secure reinforcements, Smith could reinforce Taylor with only what troops could be spared from General John B. Magruder's Texas army of less than 15,000.

Early in the year, when it became obvious that the Federals were preparing to move up the Red River in force, defenses were strengthened along the river from Shreveport to Fort DeRussy, about three miles north of Marksville. Shreveport was guarded by Forts Turnbull, Jenkins, and Albert Sidney Johnston, built at high points overlooking the west bank of the Red River, and by a dozen small batteries ringing the city. The armament of these fortifications was weak, so weak in fact that at Fort Turnbull charred logs were mounted to simulate cannon; when General Magruder inspected the fort he remarked that it was "only a hum bug," so "Fort Humbug" became its name. The steamer *New Falls City* was sunk across the channel of the Red River at the mouth of Loggy Bayou, some thirty miles down-river from Shreveport, resulting in the formation of a sand bar which effectively blocked the river.

Federal Plans for an Expedition up the Red River. The Federals hoped to occupy all of Louisiana during 1864 and perhaps even to invade eastern Texas; Shreveport, therefore, became the Federal military objective. The Republican presidential campaign of 1864 would be greatly aided if Louisiana could be brought back into the Union. The occupation of Texas was important for several reasons. That state furnished great amounts of supplies to the Confederacy, while through it flowed a considerable number of Confederate imports. Also, French strategy in Mexico hinted that Texas might become seriously involved with the new Mexican Empire now headed by Maximilian, and William H. Seward was demanding that "the flag be restored to *some one point in Texas*" to show that the United States "still owned the area." A successful campaign up the Red River would seriously weaken Confederate morale in the entire Trans-Mississippi Department and would yield large quantities of cotton, livestock, foodstuffs, and other supplies.

Just how much the American cotton situation influenced the final Federal decision to invade Central Louisiana has never been determined, but no doubt it was of paramount importance. Because of the shortage, cotton was selling at nearly $2.00 a pound in eastern cities and only about 25 per cent of all Northern spindles were in operation, while according to cautious Federal estimates, 100,000 bales waited ready for shipment at Red River landings.

General Banks supported the invasion plan, for he was led to believe that its successful culmination would greatly enhance his chances of becoming the Republican presidential candidate if there was a convention deadlock over Lincoln's candidacy. He was also heartened by General Sherman's opinion that Kirby Smith would retreat from Louisiana into Texas without a fight.

From the Mississippi to Grand Ecore. In early March, Admiral Porter assembled a large fleet of gunboats and transports at the mouth of Red River, where he was joined by General A. J. Smith with 10,000 of Sherman's troops. Fort DeRussy fell on March 14, and Porter reached Alexandria the next afternoon. General William B. Franklin arrived within a few days from the Teche Country with 15,000 infantry and several artillery batteries. General Banks reached Alexandria on the twenty-fourth, and the combined Federal army of slightly more than 30,000 men, with ample cavalry and engineers and nearly 100 field guns, was ready to invade the Red River Valley. Only General Taylor, with his small Confederate army of less than 6,000 men, stood between the advancing Federals and the Louisiana state capital.

The movement up the Red River began on March 28. The Confederates were pushed back at Henderson's Hill, at Monett's Ferry on lower Cane River, and again at Cloutierville. Natchitoches was occupied on April 1, and the Federals moved on to Grand Ecore, about four miles northward on Red River. Banks reported that he would be in Shreveport by April 10 and that he did not expect Taylor to fight; most of the other Federal generals also had "the distinct impression" that there would be no real fighting "until we got to Shreveport." Admiral Porter wrote that "the efforts of these people to keep up this war remind one very much of the antics of Chinamen, who build canvas forts, paint hideous dragons on their shields, turn somersets, and yell in the faces of their enemies to frighten them, and then run away at the first sign of an engagement. . . . It

53

Illustrations

is not the intention of these rebels to fight." Lincoln was not impressed with such optimism, however, for he commented: "I am sorry to see this tone of confidence; the next news we shall hear from there will be of a defeat."

Governor Allen had issued an eloquent appeal to the people of Louisiana. "Come, then, as did the patriotic Greeks who defied the hosts of the Persian monarch. Come as did the heroes who left their ploughs standing in the field and gathered to the defense of Rome. Come as did the men of Bruce at Bannockburn. Come as did the soldiers of Israel's king who met and conquered the Philistines." And throughout the retreat, while fighting stubborn rear-guard actions, Taylor pleaded vainly with General Kirby Smith for reinforcements so that he might turn and fight a "real battle" with the enemy. But General Banks's progress to Grand Ecore, "escorted by gun-boats and transports—saluted by cannon-discharges," had been "like that of a conqueror." Shreveport was less than a hundred miles away; the Federal army would arrive within a week.

Mansfield. There were three roads from Natchitoches to Shreveport. The Campti–Fort Towson Road ran along the east side of the Red River, while the Pleasant Hill–Mansfield Road ran at some distance west of the river. The third road closely followed the river's west bank, and would have been, as Admiral Porter wrote General Sherman, the most practical route for Banks to have taken, for "the roads are good, wide fields on all sides, a river protecting the right flank of the army, and gunboats in company." But for some reason the Federal general chose the Mansfield Road, a decision which marked the turning point of the campaign.

The Federal forces began the movement toward Shreveport on April 6, the cavalry leading the way, followed by a train of more than 300 wagons, Franklin's infantry division, the Thirteenth and Nineteenth Corps, and another train of 700 wagons. The following day, General A. J. Smith's "gorilla" divisions,* the Sixteenth Corps, the Corps d'Afrique, and a brigade of cavalry, left Grand Ecore to protect the left flank and the rear of the advancing army. Late on the afternoon of the seventh, the advance guard of the Federal army was brought to a halt after sharp skirmishes at Wilson's Farm and Carroll's Mill, about six miles north of Pleasant Hill.

That same afternoon General Taylor, near the Sabine Cross Roads, turned to General Camille Polignac and said, "Little Frenchman, I am going to fight Banks here, if he has a million of men!" Several days before, a Northern war correspondent had reported that the Confederates were concentrating their forces at Pleasant Hill, and on the fifth Banks had ordered General Franklin to force Taylor to "give battle, if possible," to march his column "with this object always in view." On the afternoon of the seventh

* So-called because of their looting of Alexandria and because the western soldiers, according to a modern Northern historian, were "coarse, uncouth, illdressed braggarts and chicken thieves."

Banks rode along the entire Federal column, now strung out on the road for several miles, apparently "pleased by what he saw." But many of his officers and men were not at all pleased with having to move along a comparatively waterless, "rugged and heavily timbered" route, through what one cavalryman called "a howling wilderness."

General Taylor had received reinforcements on the seventh. General Tom Green had arrived from Texas, Alfred Mouton's and John G. Walker's divisions were in position before Mansfield, and another force, commanded by Generals Thomas J. Churchill and Mosby M. Parsons, was protecting the Confederate rear at Keatchie.

After the skirmish at Carroll's Mill, the Confederates fell back to Sabine Cross Roads and both armies bivouacked for the night. The Confederate divisions at Keatchie were ordered to move to Mansfield the next morning. General Albert L. Lee, who commanded the Federal ten-regiment advance force, was uneasy. The Confederates had fought stubbornly at Wilson's Farm and at Carroll's Mill, the terrain was not to his liking, and it was possible that Taylor had received reinforcements. He reported his fears to Banks, was laughed at "for insisting that we would have a fight before we got to Shreveport," but was promised a brigade the next morning.

Lee moved forward on the early morning of the eighth, advancing slowly in skirmish order and using his artillery as much as the woods and the broken character of the land permitted. He advanced about six miles by noon and felt somewhat more confident that the Confederates would not make a stand, for he had passed their deserted camps with breakfast corncakes and bacon still warming over the cooking fires. General Banks reached Lee's advance position about one o'clock and could not have failed to observe the lack of proper military organization of the entire advance force and especially that the wagon train was badly located close up on the main road immediately behind the skirmishing companies, preventing quick reinforcement or immediate retreat.

During the morning, Taylor had fixed his line of battle about three miles southeast of Mansfield, behind an open field some 800 to 1,000 yards wide and 1,200 to 1,400 yards deep which extended on both sides of the road. The field sloped gradually upward to a low hill, behind which a rail fence bordered dense growths of timber ranging around three sides of the open ground. When the Federal troops emerged from the timber at the south edge of the broad, open expanse, they saw a heavy concentration of Confederates in skirmishing order extending on each side of the hill. Shortly before, Confederate soldier Arthur Hyatt had written in his diary: "The line of battle has just been formed, and we are ready and eager to meet the damned rascals."

There was some skirmishing during the early afternoon, the Federals attempting to ascertain the approximate numbers and positions of the Confederate troops, but Taylor successfully concealed the movements of his reinforcements. Shortly after four o'clock, Taylor ordered Mouton, who commanded the Confederate left wing, to begin the attack.

General Polignac's command was made up largely of Texans, who had never seen a Frenchman before, much less a little French prince whose full name was Camille Armand Jules Marie, Prince de Polignac. His name had irreverent possibilities of ludicrous transposition, and with boisterous enthusiasm they had immediately named him "General Polecat." Polignac had said nothing about the nickname, but now, upon hearing Mouton's order, "Let us charge them right in the face, and throw them into the valley," he raised himself in his stirrups, waved his sword, and shouted: "Follow me! Follow me! You call me 'Polecat.' I will show you whether I am 'Polecat' or 'Polignac.' " And with a great shout, "yelling like infuriated demons," the Confederates charged across the open field toward the Federal right wing.

Colonel Leopold Armant of the Eighteenth Louisiana, the "Old Creole" Regiment, fell, and Colonel William Walker of the Twenty-eighth Louisiana Infantry. Seven standard-bearers of the Crescent Regiment went down "one after another with the flag." Mouton's Division lost slightly over a third of its total number killed and wounded, including its commander. Accounts differ as to the manner of Mouton's death. According to one contemporary report, he was killed by five musket balls, fired by a small group of Federal soldiers after they had surrendered and while Mouton was waving to his own men not to fire on them.

Taylor, according to one Confederate, calmly sat his horse, smoking a cigar, one leg thrown carelessly across his saddle horn, as he directed the movements of the various field units. As the attack of Mouton's Division gained momentum, Taylor ordered the Confederate right wing to move forward and turn the Federal left. The attack became general all along the line.

The Federal troops wavered, began to retreat, then panicked, and according to Confederate Theophilus Noel, "after making a desperate stand for a short time, broke in real Bull Run style." J. P. Blessington wrote that "we rushed upon the enemy before they could reload . . . and from their appearance, 'every man is for himself.' " The retreating Federal forces found the road completely blocked by wagons and mules, abandoned artillery, and cavalry horses, and soon became a "disorganized mob of screaming, sobbing, hysterical, pale, terror-stricken men." One Federal wrote that the soldiers were running "by hundreds, on foot and mounted; nor knew they scarcely why they ran, only that the rebels were coming. Then came cavalry, infantry, artillery, and wagons, crowding the road and each side." Another wrote that the mad rush included "men without hats or coats, men without guns or accoutrements, cavalrymen without horses, and artillerymen without cannon, wounded men bleeding and crying at every step, men begrimed with smoke and powder—all in a state of fear and frenzy." The battleground became a charnel field where the dead lay singly and in small clusters, in crooked windrows, caught where the fury of the Confederate charge had found them.

The Federal forces finally made a stand at Pleasant Grove, two or three miles back down the road. Night came on, a night of misery (as are all nights after a battle), broken only by the screams and moans of the wounded and the dying. During the hours of darkness Banks withdrew his army to Pleasant Hill, the road along the line of march bordered with burning wagons, worn-out stragglers, wounded men, and abandoned arms, clothing, and supplies.

The battle had been a desperately fought engagement and the losses extremely heavy. The Federals, out of a total of about 12,000 actually engaged at different stages of the fighting, had lost nearly 2,300 men, killed, wounded, missing, and captured; the Confederates, out of a total of about 8,000 engaged, lost 1,000 killed and wounded. Taylor reported that he had captured "twenty pieces of artillery, several stands of colors, many thousands of small arms, and two hundred and fifty wagons."

The Battle of Mansfield, next to the Battle of New Orleans in 1815 the greatest military engagement in Louisiana history, brought the Federal invasion of the Red River Valley to a sudden, dramatic halt. Banks had lost the battle because of an accumulation of several fatal errors and because he had permitted Taylor to choose the battle site and to surprise him. Banks had taken the wrong road to Shreveport; he had been vague in orders to subordinate officers; he had permitted his army to be strung out for a distance of some twenty miles and thus could not bring his full force to bear at the point of contact with the enemy, despite the fact that his troops outnumbered the Confederates about two and a half to one; he had given contradictory orders during the battle; and he had completely misjudged General Taylor in believing that he would not make a stand, much less order a vicious counterattack after having retreated for over two hundred miles without offering a major engagement.

Pleasant Hill. Taylor's victorious Confederates pursued the retreating Federals the following morning, April 9, and caught up with them early in the afternoon at Pleasant Hill. Posted in and about the village and for nearly a mile northward along the Mansfield Road were fresh enemy units which had not fought at Mansfield. After some maneuvering, Taylor's tired men rested about two hours. Part of his army had fought in yesterday's battle and was much jaded, while the reinforcements had arrived exhausted from marching over forty miles in thirty-six hours.

During this rest period Taylor laid careful plans. He would throw General Thomas J. Churchill, who had arrived with the reinforcing troops, against the Federal left wing. After turning the

Federals, he would send his cavalry farther around the Federal left to cut off their retreat in the direction of Natchitoches.

Churchill moved off about three in the afternoon, made contact with the enemy, and began the battle. Taylor ordered a heavy artillery bombardment of the Federal center, and about five o'clock began a general attack. Churchill pushed the Federal left center back almost into the village, while at the same time the Confederate center moved southward along the Mansfield Road, the Federals retreating in confusion.

But Churchill had not sent his cavalry far enough to his own right, and a Federal counterattack pushed him back across the ground from which he had just driven the enemy. Darkness finally put an end to the fighting. During the night the Federal army continued its retreat toward Natchitoches, while the Confederates moved back up the Mansfield Road for water and forage and went into camp.

Taylor should have won a decisive victory, but as it was, the battle ended in a draw. The Confederate failure lay in Churchill's not swinging his cavalry around far enough to the south to completely turn the Federal left wing and to occupy the Natchitoches Road. Taylor took the blame, and later explained the mistakes made, writing: "Herein lies the vast difference between genius and commonplace: one anticipates errors, the other discovers them too late."

Federal Retreat to the Mississippi. Banks claimed victory at both Mansfield and Pleasant Hill, but the majority of the Federal military and naval officers admitted defeat, Federal Colonel Duganne writing curtly: "We had lost the battle . . . the entire army was obliged to retrograde, the Red River expedition was abandoned, and our fleet and forces barely escaped annihilation at the hands of the pursuing rebels." Admiral Porter reported to Sherman that "the army has been shamefully beaten by the rebels. There is no disguising the fact. . . . Armies victorious don't often go back as this one has done."

The retreating Federal army left such destruction in its wake that the area through which it passed became known as "the burnt district," where the "track of the spoiler was one scene of desolation" and the indiscriminate destruction of property probably unsurpassed during the entire Civil War. General Taylor wrote that "the destruction of this country by the enemy exceeds anything in history." A Texas soldier described "the melancholy monuments of their devastating march. . . . Every fine residence, every corn-crib, smoke-house, cotton-gin—all that could give comfort to men—were committed to flames. Dead animals—horses, mules, cows, calves, and hogs, slain by the enemy, were scattered along the road." A Massachusetts veteran wrote that "the country was in flames. . . . It was a picture, whose equal the men had never seen before." A New Yorker admitted that "The wanton and useless destruction of property was [a] . . . lasting disgrace." Governor Allen, in one of his messages, wrote: "A painful melancholy, a death-like silence, broods over the land, and desolation reigns supreme."

Taylor pursued the retreating Federals as best he could, despite the fact that Smith had sent a large percentage of his army northward against a Federal force which had invaded Louisiana from Arkansas, but which was already retreating. Taylor had only about 5,000 men with which to harass some 25,000 Federals, who were supported by their gunboat fleet. He hit the fleet at Blair's Landing, Campti, and Grand Ecore, and attacked the Federal rear guard at Cloutierville, Monett's Ferry, and Henderson's Hill. The Federal retreat became almost a rout, covering over sixty miles to Alexandria in four days' march. Porter testified later that it was "the most perfect stampede that I ever saw in an army that was in perfect preparation to go into battle."

The Federals delayed at Alexandria a little over two weeks because the Red River had fallen so low that engineer Colonel Joseph Bailey had to build wing dams in order to get Porter's gunboats over the rapids. Meanwhile, Federal foragers scoured the countryside for cotton, cattle, hogs, horses, mules, foodstuffs, and forage for animals, stripping homes in the process and "confiscating" anything that attracted their eyes. On May 3, for example, a forage train of 100 wagons "gathered supplies" at Governor Moore's plantation. Animals were butchered in the streets of Alexandria, and the remains were left to "decay in the summer sun, till the whole atmosphere became impregnated with a disgusting and sickening odor. Millions of flies filled the streets like an Egyptian plague."

The Federal army moved out of Alexandria on May 13. Despite specific orders and precautions by General Banks, the city was fired; other Federal officers were not so considerate, and it was reported that General A. J. Smith said, as he looked back at the burning city, "Boys, this *looks like war!*" A correspondent of a St. Louis newspaper wrote that "some of the soldiers, both white and black, as if by general understanding, set fire to the city in nearly every part, almost simultaneously." Looting by soldiers and civilians with the Federal army accompanied the fire. Lawrence Van Alstyne wrote that "there is no use trying to tell about the sights I saw and the sounds of distress I heard. It cannot be told and could hardly be believed if it were told." By noon the city was nine-tenths destroyed—"all the business parts and all the fine residences, the Ice House Hotel, the Court House [whose wills, successions, suit records, transfers of property, mortgages, and other archives dated back to the middle of the eighteenth century], all the churches except the Catholic . . . and the entire front row of large and splendid business houses."

Many Federal soldiers later testified that the retreat from Alexandria became a near rout. Van Alstyne, for example, wrote that on the sixteenth, after having been on the move from 3:30 A.M. until midnight, there "began such marching as we never before had done. No attention was paid to the files. Those that could keep up did so, and the rest fell out by the way." Five days later he wrote that the soldiers were "dropping like dead men, and it was impossible to rouse them from the deathlike sleep that had overtaken them." One Union captain reported that "longer and more rapid forced marches than this of ours have been made, but I am glad that I was not called upon to assist at the performance."

Taylor and his depleted Confederate army closed in on the rapidly retreating Federals. He hit them at Wilson's Landing on the fourteenth, at Marksville on the fifteenth, at Mansura on the sixteenth, and at Moreauville on the seventeenth, and vainly attempted to halt them at Yellow Bayou and Bayou De Glaize on the eighteenth. The road to Simmesport on the Atchafalaya, and to the protection of the heavy Mississippi River gunboat fleet, was now open. The Red River Campaign had ended. Banks was back where he had started nearly two and a half months before.

Results of the Campaign. Modern writer H. L. Landers has concluded that "no campaign of the Civil War produced so prolific a crop of poisonous quarrels as did this one." The charges and countercharges continued until the deaths of those concerned. On May 18, Confederate General Taylor wrote that only the depleting of his forces by General E. Kirby Smith, who had sent several of Taylor's divisions to Arkansas, had "prevented the capture of Banks's army and the destruction of Porter's fleet. I feel bitterly about this, because my army has been robbed of the just measure of its glory and the country of the most brilliant and complete success of the war." Smith was certainly at odds with Taylor, for in his congratulatory message to the army after the two battles he did not mention Taylor's name. Taylor asked to be relieved from further service under Smith and was soon given command of the Department of Alabama, Mississippi, and East Louisiana. The story of the Red River Campaign might well have had a different conclusion if Taylor had been in command of the Confederate forces in Louisiana.

The Federal Committee on the Conduct of the War held a full-scale investigation which accomplished little except to bring out the fact that the Federal commanders had been almost completely incompatible, that the expedition had been ordered from Washington, and that, as General T. Kilby Smith testified, it was "what would be called in military parlance a mercantile expedition." A comparatively large number of civilians had accompanied the expedition, upon the authority of President Abraham Lincoln, apparently for the purpose of trading in cotton, and the gunboat fleet had confiscated so much cotton that Banks's aide reported that the stamps "C.S.A." and "U.S.N." meant "Cotton Stealing Association of the United States Navy." The Federal government soon incorporated the Department of the Gulf into the Military Division of West Mississippi, under the command of General E. R. S. Canby, and Banks was replaced by General Stephen A. Hurlbut. Porter never lived down the Confederate charge that he was "The Thief of the Mississippi" and even found it necessary to explain to his own mother that the cabin of his gunboat was *not* "full of silver taken from the plantations," while Banks had the unique distinction of being "hooted at" by his own men.

Military Operations After the Red River Campaign. Major Federal military operations for 1864 ended with the closing of the Red River Campaign in May. During the rest of the year small bodies of Federal troops were dispatched from troop-concentration points at Lake Providence, Vidalia, Baton Rouge, Port Hudson, Morganza, and Brashear City on raids into nearby areas of northeastern and southeastern Louisiana and into the Florida Parishes. During the late summer, Captain Joseph C. Lee led a Confederate force against the Federals along the west side of the Mississippi north of the Red River and was later attacked by Federal Major C. H. Chapin, who commanded a detachment of Negro troops. In October, Federal General Albert L. Lee raided northeastward from Baton Rouge into southern Mississippi, stripping the country of livestock and food supplies, capturing a few prisoners, and burning large amounts of cotton.

But with these exceptions, there was little Federal military activity. For those Louisiana civilians who lived in any of the sections that had been in the path of Federal troops, the main problem was to obtain sustenance enough to stay alive.

VIII

Soldier Life with Johnny Reb of Louisiana

Louisiana's Johnny Reb. Louisiana's average Johnny Reb belonged to no special category of the body politic. He was poor, wealthy, or just middle class; was French, Spanish, German, Irish, or one of over thirty other nationalities or a mixture of several of them; was a farmer, mechanic, gambler, dancing master, apothecary, overseer, teacher, or a member of one of a hundred other occupational groups. He was comparatively young and sometimes had not yet even begun to shave, although some of his comrades were over sixty. He usually lacked social polish and much formal education, and although generally he could read, he not infrequently wrote without benefit of capitalization or punctuation.

He knew fear and sometimes panic in his first battle but adopted the motto: "Bein' scared's all right. Backin' away ain't." Soon he came to believe that for him Death had taken a holiday, or simply that every soldier had a rendezvous with Death: "Meet it today and you don't have to meet it tomorrow." He spoke many languages, though his non-English specialities were French, Spanish, and German. If he was a Creole, he frequently was not much for size and so was called "rooster," "bantam," "gamecock," and other fowlish names by Anglo-Saxon comrades.

He would have agreed with "Stonewall" Jackson that "War means fighting. The business of the soldier is to fight." He knew that his own valor would pass unnoticed except by close comrades, that probably he would "be touched by the finger of God" and would occupy a nameless grave on some bleak hillside; for he had vainly searched for friends when the companies re-formed after battles, and he remembered that the crack of his own rifle and the whine of his own bullet had sung death songs across the smoke-filled hell of the battlefield. But he had dedicated himself to the bleak, monotonous, monastic life of a soldier, and his "coin rang soundly on the marble counter-top." He was proud to do his duty, but thought frequently of his wife and his children, his guarantee of personal immortality should he fall in battle. He well knew that he was expected to be a good soldier; after the war Sarah Dorsey wrote:

63

"We don't think the Southern men deserve so much credit for *fighting well*—that was to be expected of such a race as ours."

As he campaigned and fought battle after battle, he changed from the soft, well-filled-out civilian to the tough, gaunt, even emaciated, veteran. He seemingly was made of half-human rawhide and gristle, with nerves tightly drawn, with the skin of the forehead and cheeks stretched tight, too tight. His deep-sunken eyes generally roved up and down, side to side, as though they were doing guard duty in a dense forest at midnight, trying to pierce like the eyes of a cat the blankness of black; but even when still the eyes were aware, very much aware. His movements might be either slow and languid or quick and deliberate; and he sometimes had a soft, gliding gait, putting his feet down flat, carefully, and then sliding his weight forward easily onto them.

He had learned his lessons and tricks of soldiering well. If he were a sharpshooter, he had learned how to steady his rifle sight, drawing the deep breath and then letting it halfway out, relaxing the entire body so that not a single muscle was tense, especially in the chest, for even one tense muscle would cause the gun to waver and the shot to be missed, and the precious powder and bullet to be fired for nothing. If he were a cavalryman, he had learned to swing his saber easily in left and right moulinets, thrusts, and slashes. He had learned as an infantryman during the bitter cold of Border State winter to pass the night-guard hours tightening and then loosening the muscles of the legs, then the arms, then the back, the chest, and the belly, to keep the blood flowing slowly and steadily and so to keep from freezing.

He had learned to control the fears of advance posts, where every shadow concealed death, where loneliness beat upon him until he got the notion that a thousand listening ears surrounded him and that a whole platoon was rushing toward him with fixed bayonets. He had learned that there was a time for patience and also a time for audacity. He had learned to take the few, sometimes forced, amusements of the soldier and make the most of them; for although as a soldier he was a tireless assemblage of bone and flesh and hide and iron-willed resolution, he was still a man and not a machine. He had learned to be a quiet man of long silences, for he had known the silence of loneliness for a long time and he had built a tight little world of stoic tragedy completely around his heart, where he was slowly starving. As Robert Patrick once wrote: "I felt dejected and heartsick as I wandered over those cold, barren, cheerless hills. The wind sighed along in mournful cadences, through the dismantled forest trees and over the rugged hilltops, and I could not help thinking of the comforts of home and all its pleasures when I contemplated this desolate scene."

Discipline and Morale. A noted Southern historian has written that the Confederate soldier was unsurpassable only when commanded by officers who maintained strict discipline and who possessed a deep understanding of the rear-rank buck private's individual pride. Immediately following a heroic battle performance, the soldier sometimes tended to evade drill, feign sickness, neglect his uniform and equipment, and to be disrespectful and even surly to superiors. But pride in one's outfit, *esprit de corps*, and strong morale eventually came to most such soldiers. The Nineteenth Louisiana Regiment at the Battle of Chickamauga lost 40 per cent of the 349 men who went into the fight.

Regulations for the individual soldier's conduct included a long list of prohibitions: absence without leave, insubordination, disrespect to officers, turbulence after taps, missing roll call, slovenly personal appearance, poor care of weapons, sleeping while on guard duty, and many others. Punishments were sometimes ingeniously devised: bucking and gagging (sitting, hands bound, elbows placed under a stick thrust under the knees), doing knapsack drill (with the knapsack filled with stones or bricks), sitting in a sweatbox, riding a wooden horse, carrying a heavy log, or wearing the wooden overcoat (holding up a wooden barrel which had one or both ends knocked out). For serious offenses or crimes the penalty might be execution by a firing squad, the prisoner sometimes sitting on his own coffin by the side of the open grave.

Many soldiers, however, received lenient treatment from understanding officers of military courts. When Private C. A. Everett of the Washington Artillery, for example, was tried for sleeping on picket duty he was sentenced to only three days' confinement in the guardhouse with bread-and-water rations. The court noted that Everett had displayed proper "penitence for consciousness of the grievousness of the offence" and "that on the night and time stated in the charge the accused had been induced to partake of an extraordinary quantity of liquor to which he was not accustomed."

Clothing and Shelter. Johnny Reb was usually sent off to war with considerable neighborhood enthusiasm. He attended farewell balls, picnics, parties, and *tableaux vivants* where he thrilled to elaborate posturings titled "The Goddess of Liberty," "The Confederate States," "The Nine Muses," and perhaps a scene showing Isabella presenting her jewels to Columbus. His gifts included everything from flags to frying pans to heavy blankets with "pockets at the top for soap, combs, brushes, handkerchiefs, etc."

His neighbors frequently uniformed him for the parade ground rather than for the battlefield in suits of blue, green, yellow, or even flaming red. The Orleans Guards, for example, arrived at the battlefield of Shiloh dressed in blue uniforms and were immediately fired upon by less-well-costumed Confederates who took them to be Yankees; only the white linings of their coats, quickly turned inside out, saved the Guards from annihilation. The Louisiana Zouaves boasted the most "outlandish" of all uniforms, consisting of "scarlet bloomers, blue shirts, brocaded jackets, wide sashes, white gaiters, and gaudy fezzes worn at a jaunty angle."

But soon Johnny's fancy dress uniform was worn out, and then he wore whatever he could get from home, for army issues of clothing were rare after the first year of the war. If not a man of means, he wore homemade, home-dyed clothing, the colors of which sometimes ran together without pattern, clothing which was soon filled with Johnny's own multicolored darns and patches.

If cleanliness made a man godly, Johnny was no saint, for he was dirty most of the time. Lack of soap and laundry facilities made it impossible to keep his person or his clothing clean. Occasionally, when there was time and a stream near at hand, he gave his coat, pants, and shirt a "Confederate Military Wash"—tying them to a bush at the water's edge, allowing them to soak for a considerable time, then stirring them with a stick or beating them on a rock, and finally hanging them on a bush to dry. If he had had the opportunity to boil his clothing, he became the object of considerable jesting; comrades would carefully examine his shirt front and then, striking an exaggerated pose, exclaim, "Biled, by Jove." But most of the time he lived without benefit of the frequent use of soap and water, and the smells of the "long, hot days of sour-turned sweat and rancid body vinegar" were not soon forgotten.

The men performed hair-styling miracles and cunningly devised mustaches and whiskers of outlandish design which would have caused consternation in the tonsorial parlors of New Orleans. A finely twisted, tight mustache generally elicited such remarks as "Take them mice out'er your mouth; take 'em out; no use to say they aint thar; see their tails hangin' out"; while a well-grown beard called for "come out from that bunch of hair. I know you're there. I see your ears a workin'."

When in the field, officers below the rank of general were housed in tents large enough for ten to twelve men while privates and noncommissioned officers bunked two or four to a tent; by the end of the second year of the war, however, tents were becoming scarce for armies on the move. When he could settle down in one place for a spell, Johnny Reb showed considerable ingenuity in the construction of housing, utilizing blankets, earth, wooden boards, captured rubber cloth, bark, leaves, logs, moss, clay, canvas, tin—literally anything that would halfway protect him from the elements. He burrowed into hillsides, built half-in-half-out-of-the-ground dugouts, bored "gopher holes" and covered them with poles and earth or with his tent, and occasionally had time to erect log cabins. In general, he was a poorly sheltered soldier, constantly attacked in winter by cold and rain, snow and ice and sleet, and so was vulnerable to numerous chest and throat diseases.

Confederate Cuisine. The Louisiana soldier generally complained of army rations, with good reason, for he was poorly fed. He commonly joined with several comrades to form a "mess," and took his regular turn with cooking pot and frying pan. He was always hungry for salt, pepper, and sugar, and if he came from the southern section of the state, begged the home folks to send him, as one private wrote, "a strong bottle of strong pepper sauce or some good, strong catsup."

The most common food issues were corn meal and salted or smoked beef or pork, much of which was of poor quality, wormy, or even spoiled. Lieutenant Howell Carter wrote that the test for genuine "pure *blue* beef" was that the cow had been unable to "step or jump" over a rail fence let down to the fourth rail.

Like other Confederates, he soon learned to exist on practically any type of foodstuffs and to march long distances on a single "Confederate Sandwich"—a "corndodger split and with only a thin slice of bacon between the pieces." But necessity did not always mean cheery acceptance of such fare. Just before Robert E. Lee's surrender one veteran wrote that "if any person offers me cornbread after this war comes to a close I shall *probably* tell him to—go to hell." Young Robert Patrick once complained that "I am sick and tired of grease, grease, grease. It keeps my thoughts by day and my dreams by night." John Ellis wrote his mother that "when I see dirt in my victuals, I take it out and eat on. If I taste it, I swallow and eat on. If my coffee is not strong, I thank the Lord that it is as strong as it is & drink it." Horse and mule meat was sometimes issued as "beef," and one soldier wrote that "I have seen bones in meat that I well know never grew in a cow, or a steer."

Captured Federal army rations fed many a famished Confederate after a victory or successful raid. It was common knowledge that "the Yankees had everything" including "mixed vegetables pressed and hermetically sealed. . . . Coffee, concentrated milk and sugar in the same way." One Louisiana soldier could "hardly conceive how well *their armies* are supplied and how poorly *ours.*" However, there were short periods when men like Fred Taber could write that they were eating loaf bread and fresh beef and Sergeant William H. Tunnard could report that Christmas dinner in 1864 consisted of "fine roast turkey, light bread and butter, potatoes, pies, cake and coffee." Such Epicurean festive dinners were usually preceded by eggnog or other spiritous concoctions, or perhaps by straight whiskey, nicknamed "Bust Skull," "Old Red Eye," "Tanglefoot," "Rifle Knock-Knee," or "Rock Me To Sleep, Mother."

Soldier Complaints. If the old adage that "a complaining soldier is a good soldier" is true, then Johnny Reb was indeed a good fighting man, for he aired his real or imagined grievances about everyone and everything. On November 6, 1864, for example, Robert Patrick's cup of woe ran over:

I am annoyed by several little things and I am out of humor. The weather is so bad that it is enough to give any man the blues; my tent is knee deep in mud and water and the smoke almost put my eyes out; I am hungry, for I have not had anything to eat since morning and when night comes I must roll down in the mud. On top of the whole of it I have just learned that old Lincoln has been re-elected to the presidency. Well I suppose that we are in for four years more.

Soldiers complained about snakes, rains ("there was a general uncorking among the clouds"), lice, bugs, mosquitoes, food, military regulations, officers from the rank of corporal to army-commanding generals, blistered feet ("I do not mean a single blister, as big as a pea, but a series of blisters, each as large as a dollar"), clothing, weight of knapsacks, not receiving pay ("we have drawn no money now for nearly 7 months"), drinking whiskey when on the march ("you go better for a few minutes, and then you are worse off than ever"), dust, lack of medicines, and a hundred other things. Louisianians did not like the colder temperatures of the northern areas of the South, and Captain Arthur W. Hyatt wrote on New Year's Day, 1864, that it was "really pitiable" to see the men "sitting around their fires, nodding and almost asleep" the ground being "too cold for them to lie down upon."

Rains and storms were objects of comment in diaries or in letters home. One soldier wrote that "rain is good or bad, according to circumstances. In hot weather it cools the skin, invigorates the muscles, and is a positive comfort," but when marching it "is greater nuisance than people in carriages would imagine." One Louisiana "butternut," after marching all day while the rain poured down "in sheets," finally sat down to spend a miserable night: "As I sat on my knapsack, it settled down into the mud until it just kept me out of the pool. My boots sank into the mud half-way to the tops. I rested my elbows on my knees, and chewed the cud of misery." And more than one soldier was well acquainted with the lines:

> Now I lay me down to sleep
> In mud that's many fathoms deep;
> If I'm not here when you awake,
> Just hunt me up with an oyster rake.

Body lice did not cause too much trouble, for "we just boiled our clothes and that's the end of them," but between stops long enough to boil clothing the vermin "roamed over the anatomy at large." They were given a great variety of grimly jocular names, such as "Graybacks," "Zouaves," "Tigers," "Bragg's Bodyguard," and their extermination was frequently referred to in military terms. Killing them was called "fighting under the black flag"; turning a shirt inside out was termed "executing a flank movement"; while discarding a garment was called "giving the vermin a parole." Mosquitoes were a special problem, and one Louisianian wrote graphicly from Virginia that reveille was not necessary, for "the microscopic feet and inquisitive suckers of an army numerous as the sands of the sea shore will awaken a regiment of men from innocent sleep to wide-awake profanity." A small black bug, according to one veteran, delighted to crawl into the ears of sleeping soldiers—"They make a man raving crazy. The doctors pour oil in first, and then syringe them out. Nearly every night there is a bug case."

Disease and Battle Wounds. The enlistee or drafted man had been given an alleged medical examination, but there were few ills or deformities serious enough to prevent his being accepted as a soldier. Deafness, speech impediment, "general debility," "functional heart trouble," epilepsy, rheumatism, "slight deformity," loss of one eye or one or two fingers, myopia, hernia, hemorrhoids, and numerous other ills, "unless excessive," were not deemed sufficient cause to exempt him from military service. So he marched off to war, where constant exposure, badly prepared food, lack of balanced diet, insufficient shelter, lack of ordinary sanitation facilities, and extreme physical exertion made him susceptible to epidemic, infectious, endemic, and other types of diseases.

Dr. Joseph Jones, one of the most outstanding Confederate medical officers, estimated that the average soldier fell victim to wounds or disease six times during the course of the war, that approximately one third of all Southern soldiers died of disease or wounds or were killed outright in battle, and that three times as many died of disease as were killed in battle or died of wounds. The ranks were never completely filled. One company officer wrote during the summer of 1863 that only slightly more than a dozen men were able to answer roll call or to attend dress parade, and John Ellis once reported that from his company "21 have died of disease, 18 have become so unhealthy as to be discharged, and only four have been killed in battle." A cavalry brigade commander reported late in 1862 that of a total of 2,319 men only 1,068 were fit for duty.

While most of a soldier's ailments were digestive or respiratory in nature, he was subject to "all the ills that human flesh is heir to." He suffered from diarrhea, dysentery, bronchitis, typhoid fever, pneumonia, measles, malaria, "chills and fever," typhus fever, smallpox, scarlet fever, various types of ulcers, tuberculosis, "debilitas," catarrh, rheumatism, scurvy, "camp itch," colic, indigestion, frostbite, glandular swellings, and many others. In some cases he was "laid up" for only a few days; in others, he was ill for weeks and then "made slow recovery" or "came under the Finger of God."

All manner of drugs and medicinal concoctions were prescribed for his ills: "Blue Mass," quinine, "Georgia Bark," calomel, opium, iodine, chloroform, rosemary, sweet gum, turpentine, alcohol, whiskey, acetate of lead, "Diseremus Pills," "Fodder Tea," "Diarrhoea Mixture," "Dovers Powders," red-pepper and resin pills, and numerous others. But the supply of drugs was never adequate, and many a fighting man fell victim to disease because of the absence of ordinary medicines.

While medical officers faced almost overwhelming odds in lack of sufficient medicines, field hospitals, clothing, dressings and bandages, nurses, and adequate food for bedridden or ambulatory patients, many soldiers had little faith in company doctors. Certainly some of their prescribings amazed their patients; when Colonel J. O. Nixon of the First Louisiana Cavalry fell ill with chills and fever, the doctor said that the only medicines he had were "calomel, blue-mass, dovers-powders, quinine and whiskey, and I am going to give you some of all." Another soldier reported that a patient was first given a large dose of calomel, then "dose after dose of quinine and other strong medicines until they either kill the individual or ruin his constitution."

Before a battle the "Infirmary Corps" of each regiment made careful preparations for tending the wounded. Corps members checked supplies of surgical instruments, needles, pins, ligatures, chloroform, alcoholic stimulants, morphine, tourniquets, bandages, lint, splints, canteens of water, and other necessities. During the battle they ministered as much as possible to the wounded men on the field; afterwards the wounded were brought to field hospitals. Operating tables were improvised—the tail gate of a wagon, boards or doors laid upon barrels or boxes, "the communion table of a church"—and they were soon "slimy with blood," for patient followed patient "in constant stream." The battlefield was a terrible place, and after Gettysburg one soldier wrote: "This is a horrid night, cold and wet and rainy. Groans and shrieks and maniacal ravings; bitter sobs, and heavy sighs, piteous cries; horrid oaths; despair, the death rattle, darkness; death."

Religion. The Louisiana soldier, like Confederates from other states and soldiers of the Union, went into battle with varying emotions—most often, probably, with curses on his lips and with hatred in his eyes. After the guns became silent, he returned to the battleground to search for and bury the bodies of comrades—and perhaps to pray. And so he stood upon the silent field, among the companions who had gone on ahead and who would be living memories for years to come, or with those still alive but worn-out, old before their time, drained dry by the long days and weeks and months of following the colors.

The dead were all around him, some lying in grotesque positions, some peaceful, others with their rifles still stoutly held, facing the front where the Stars and Bars had gone. Some could be identified, not by looking at the dirty, blackened face, but by some small trinket worn or kept in a pocket, something which had meant so much to the living man. The grave would be dug, the body laid to rest, and then covered with the soil of the South. And on a small board, if one was available, might be written a few brief words: "Broussard, John Pendleton, Sergeant, Company F., 19th Louisiana Infantry, from duty to deceased, about noon, July 16, 1863."

It was moments like this which brought the soldier face to face with the fact that he was living on borrowed time, and so, perhaps, he turned to religion for peace of mind, for that calm stoicism in the face of death which every soldier must have.

According to historian Sidney J. Romero, all ministers who

served in the Confederate forces may be grouped into one of three divisions: " . . . those who took part in actual combat, serving from within the ranks, those who were sponsored by their churches to serve as missionaries or acting chaplains, and those who were commissioned chaplain by the Confederate States of America." The list of prominent Louisiana churchmen who served in the army is impressive. General Leonidas Polk, Bishop of the Protestant Episcopal Diocese of Louisiana, was killed at Pine Mountain, Georgia. Jesuit Father Darius Hubert, who had blessed the Louisiana flag immediately after the Secession Convention had voted Louisiana out of the Union, chaplain of the First Louisiana Volunteers, went with his men into every battle and was wounded during Pickett's charge at Gettysburg. Father Antoine de Chaignon and Father François Turgis were both wounded at Shiloh. The Reverend B. M. Palmer, famed Presbyterian minister who had preached the noted Thanksgiving Day sermon in 1860, never became a chaplain but as a missionary moved about, preaching and doing "all the good" he could. The Reverend Thomas R. Markham, after having enlisted as a private in the Confederate Guards, was appointed to a chaplaincy and served at the siege of Vicksburg and in the Georgia campaigns of Joseph E. Johnston and John B. Hood.

Ordained and unordained officers preached to companies and regiments, Bishop-General Leonidas Polk in the spring of 1864 baptized Generals Hood, William J. Hardee, and Johnston, and on several occasions an Englishman serving with the Army of Northern Virginia saw "General Beauregard and other officers kneeling with scores of privates at the Holy Communion Table." Protestant revivals were common and a soldier once wrote from Minden that over 250 men had been converted from his division alone. Protestants did much hymn singing, and Catholics frequently joined them in singing "Rock of Ages," "Jesus, Lover of My Soul," "Nearer My God to Thee," and other old hymns. That religion meant much to the soldier is evidenced in many of his diary entries and letters to folks at home.

Amusements. Soldiering was generally a very dull job, and as historian Bell I. Wiley has written, "the long hours in camp were wont to bear heavily on the Confederate private." But Johnny Reb was a very sociable person and, if he came from Louisiana, frequently possessed somewhat more sociability and lighthearted "explosiveness" than many of his comrades, for he was in a number of respects a completely irrepressible man.

The Louisiana soldier loved music and so he sang popular songs of the day, ballads of foreign origin, Protestant hymns, snatches of Catholic masses, arias from the world's great operas, and marching patters, some of which were of his own composing. He bought songbooks and sheet music published by Blackmar, Werlein, or some other New Orleans firm and played in bands and in what today would be called jazz orchestras.

Among his favorite songs were "Home, Sweet Home," "Lorena,"

"All Quiet Along the Potomac Tonight," "Annie Laurie," and "Just Before the Battle, Mother." He loved "Dixie" with strong passion, just as he loved the French-Spanish-American songs and ballads of his own particular section of Louisiana. He wrote parodies of "practically everything," one of which, "I Wish I Was In Richmond," was introduced by the Bienville Rifles as they entrained for the Confederate capital in 1861.

He improvised musical instruments, generally of the percussion or string variety, and ignored proper instrumentation of his musical groups. Kennedy's Louisiana Battalion Minstrel Band, for example, which played concerts and also provided music for parades, for reviews, and for camp "hoe-downs," had a few instruments extremely difficult to classify. One of them was the "Cross Fiddle," made of a drumhead "nailed over half a whiskey keg with a rough pine neck, and strings and screws accordin'." General Leonidas Polk's Brigade Band was composed of "one cornet, one bass horn, two violins, two flutes, and one guitar." But any rendition of music was appreciated, and one soldier wrote sentimentally after hearing a band play "Shells of Ocean": "As the familiar notes of this sweet air are gently wafted in delightful cadences over the woody hills and dewy fields of the quiet forest, numberless visions of home in happier hours and sweet reminiscences of the past crowd thick and fast upon my soul and bring to view a green spot on memory's wide waste."

All kinds of sports were enjoyed whenever possible and included baseball, cricket, foot racing, boxing, marbles, leapfrog, football, "hot Jackets" (two men whipped each other with switches), tenpins (they sometimes used cannon balls), and hunting and fishing. Cavalry units organized ring tournaments and raced horses. Roach and louse races were extremely popular and not infrequently were accompanied by large bets. Card playing was universal, and games of "Twenty-one," "Poker," "Chuck-a-luck," and "Seven-up" were to be found in every large encampment twenty-four hours of the day. Frank Richardson wrote that he had seen men on the battlefield play poker "while resting for a charge."

Amateur theatricals were common, and a few thespian groups gained wide army reputations. During the first two years of the war, plays and variety shows were sometimes elaborately staged, even to colorful costumes and printed programs. Early in 1863, one theatrical program of the Washington Artillery included the play "Pocahontas, Ye Gentle Savage," an afterpiece called "Toodles," and for the closing the band's enthusiastic rendition of "The Bonnie Blue Flag." William Miller Owen wrote that "the house came down any number of times and the audience appeared delighted."

The Louisianian also had a fondness for horseplay. He "accidentally" bumped comrades against trees, pushed them into ditches or ravines, and shoved them into patches of briars or against thorny vines. Tenderfeet were rolled in mud or tossed into streams or ponds. Stove chimneys were stopped up and firewood sometimes loaded with gunpowder. A new recruit was frequently placed on picket duty with an unloaded gun, whereupon his comrades charged his position with bloodcurdling yells; if he fled the scene it was "considered a capital joke." Companies and regiments from different states sometimes engaged in snowball fights. When one Louisiana outfit won a hard-fought engagement with a Georgia company, a participant reported that "Capt C H Slocomb lost two front teeth —Lieut Challeron a blackeye—Among the Privates of the 5th Co was 5 bloody noses a[nd] a Blackeye—all of them more or less bruised among the captured property is the flag of the Ga Regiment 8 or 10 caps and Hats 1 frying pan and 4 or 5 pones of corn bread."

Days of a Soldier—And the Man. Such a composite man was the Louisiana Confederate soldier and such were some of the facets of his soldier life during the 1860's. He was a typical north or south Louisiana country-born or city-bred boy or man who was simply doing his duty as a citizen, and only occasionally did he show a yellow streak. He loved Louisiana, whether he came from New Orleans or Shreveport, or the rolling country of the Driskill Mountains, or the prairies of Opelousas, Mamou, and the Atakapas, or the land of the trembling marshes, or the rich banks of Bayou Lafourche, Bayou Macon, Saline Bayou, Bogue Chitto, or Bayou D'Arbonne.

He was not a perfect man, indeed he was far from it, but he was a man. He had gone to war with lightheartedness and with strong belief in a speedy victory and a triumphant return home; not long afterward he realized that the way would be long and hard and as time passed he became increasingly nostalgic, war-weary, fatalistic. He proved that he was a good fighting man, fighting where fighting didn't just mean shooting a rifle but fighting straight and steady, stubborn and bullheaded-like, through all his days as a soldier, through an existence that was big and little, decent and mean, and sometimes gallant and glorious.

So Johnny Reb from Louisiana lived the days and years of his life as a Confederate soldier, expecting the death which perhaps never came, drilling and marching, and fighting, and advancing and retreating, and grousing and griping, and playing jokes and laughing, and then fighting again. That he made a record of which he and his descendants could be proud, that he wrote his name and his achievements with indelible colors across the pages of history, has been established by the merciless and awful judgments of time.

IX

1865—The End of the War

"Our Race Is About Run." On the sixth of June, 1864, young
Robert Patrick wrote in his diary: "Now I will make a prophesy
and time will tell whether or not it will be correct. I think that
there will be no more fighting after June 1, 1865; that the tale will
be told one way or another." Robert missed by one day, for on June
2, 1865, the official surrender papers of the Trans-Mississippi Department were signed, marking the end of the War for Southern
Independence.

By the beginning of 1865 the South was exhausted, even the
army of General Robert E. Lee in Virginia could not be adequately
reinforced or supplied. The North had roughly three times the
white population of the South, ten times the industrial workers, two
and one-half times the miles of railroad track and five times the
rolling stock, nearly six times the banking capital, and enlisted or
drafted about two times the number of soldiers. From this vast
reservoir of men and supplies Grant made constant requisition—he
had only to grunt and the earth shook with the tread of marching,
well-equipped reinforcements, to nod and new batteries wheeled
into line, to wave his hand and troops of fresh cavalry galloped
past. With a numerical advantage of six to one he "ground Lee to
powder," not through battlefield genius but through sheer power, a
heavyweight taking the futile blows of a worn-out bantamweight
and waiting to deliver the one knockout punch. The Old Imperial
South had been beaten to its knees—to a man upon his knees every
attacker is a giant.

There was no hope in Louisiana, for her eastern and southeastern sections were held by Federal armies and Kirby Smith's forces
were not strong enough to attack them. The fighting war had ended
after the ignominious retreat of General Banks down the Red River
in May, 1864. From this time on the United States took little military interest in the Confederate Trans-Mississippi Department.

Kirby Smith reorganized his Department, but made no major
attempt to dislodge the Federal forces. General John G. Walker su-
perseded Taylor as commander of the District of Louisiana in early

June, 1864, and Walker was followed by General Simon B. Buckner two months later. At the beginning of 1865, Smith commanded a total of about 60,000 troops, but less than 15,000 of them were in Louisiana, concentrated at Minden, Shreveport, Alexandria, and Opelousas.

During the early months of 1865 there was considerable activity by small Federal and Confederate raiding parties in southeastern Louisiana, and skirmishes were fought at or near Plaquemine, Donaldsonville, Thibodaux, Brashear City, Grosse Tete, Morganza, Bayou Goula, Lake Verret, Clinton, Baton Rouge, and along Bayou Teche. In early February, Federal Colonel E. D. Osband led about 3,000 well-mounted and well-equipped cavalry into northeast Louisiana to attack Colonel Isaac F. Harrison's small Confederate force which had been causing the Federals considerable discomfiture. Foiled in this objective when Harrison withdrew westward across the Ouachita, the Federals contented themselves with winning small engagements at Oak Ridge, Bastrop, Mer Rouge, and Monroe, and with destroying or carrying off tremendous quantities of supplies and livestock. Osband reported that he had wrought "considerable destruction in the area" and that "the people have neither seed, corn, nor bread, or the mills to grind the corn in if they had it." At the Spyker family's "New Hope" plantation in Morehouse Parish, for example, the soldiers "amused themselves by killing sheep, hogs and cattle, and testing their skill in sabre practice by cutting off the heads of turkeys and chickens at a single stroke," burned several outbuildings, and ransacked the house.

Many Louisianians, who were highly critical of Kirby Smith and the Confederate government, felt they had been forgotten; comparatively few realized that conditions were pretty generally the same throughout the South and that in many respects the troops west of the Mississippi were even better supplied than were the soldiers of Johnston and Lee.

Decline of Military and Civilian Morale. Civilian as well as military morale sharply declined after the opening of the new year. Many civilians had lost loved ones, had been driven from their homes, and were now living in penury and want. Some soldiers were recent draftees who had never seen a battle; others were "fair-weather" patriots, "snowbirds" ready to desert at the first sign of hardship, or weaklings quick to fall out along the road or to drop behind shelter during a charge.

On February 12, Frank Palms wrote from Alexandria to Henrietta Lauzin of Baton Rouge that the "Missouri and Ark. troops are deserting daily and going home." Two weeks later he admitted that "the state of things now in this Dept. approaches nearer to mutiny than anything I can say." By the first of April local government began to break down and "depredations and robberies" were reported in many sections of the state. Sergeant William H. Tunnard of the Third Louisiana Infantry wrote from Shreveport that there was much excitement "over the constant reverses befalling the Confederate armies."

Many of the "folks at home" hung on with stubborn, grim determination and with forced gaiety that temporarily drove away the gathering gloom. On February 18, for example, some 15,000 citizens of Bossier and Caddo parishes held a "grand festival and barbecue" in honor of General John H. Forney's division, which had been ordered to east Texas. Sergeant Tunnard wrote that a troop inspection and a sham battle were featured at the occasion.

Then the news of Lee's surrender broke like a tidal wave over the South. In Louisiana, first came disbelief, then fleeting resolutions of courage and defiance, then reactions of timidity and despair. Kate Stone wrote in her diary that most people now thought it "useless to struggle longer." Others believed that there "was no more cause. No more struggle, no more government, no more armed resistance." But in many sections of the state men hid horses in the swamps and in the forests in the hope that Jefferson Davis might yet come westward to lead the fight "to the last extremity."

Then the bells tolled, even in Confederate Louisiana, announcing the death of Abraham Lincoln. Some "shuddered, not knowing what turn vengeance might take," for they felt that "the weight of the responsibility would fall on all adherents of the Confederacy." Colonel James M. Morgan later wrote that Lincoln's assassination was "the greatest misfortune that happened to the South." Another soldier, writing some years after the war, wondered if "all the misery, pillage and degradation which the South endured through eight years of Grantism and reconstruction would not have been saved her if the miserable assassin had stayed his hand and permitted Abraham Lincoln to live."

Disintegration of the Army. Desertions gradually increased during January, February, and March, and after the surrender of Lee and Johnston they became epidemic. On April 24, Kirby Smith's stirring appeal to the soldiers of the Trans-Mississippi Department was read to the troops on dress parade at Shreveport: "The crisis of our revolution is at hand. Great disasters have overtaken us. . . . With you rest the hopes of our nation, and upon your action depends the fate of our people. . . . Stand by your colors—maintain your discipline." But a Federal spy reported that the appeal had little effect upon the troops and that "the Army of the Trans-Mississippi was in spirit crushed."

General Buckner begged Governor Allen to come to Natchitoches to address the demoralized and disheartened troops. In answer to Allen's pathetic pleas to a division near Mansfield, the men promised to stand firm, but many forgot their promises after he departed. He returned to Shreveport and called a public mass meeting on April 29 to consider "the wants and conditions of the country," and to suggest measures "necessary to encourage our people and promote the success of our Glorious cause." Thousands of civil officials, military officers, soldiers, and civilians came, and "the exercises continued from eleven in the morning until after four in the afternoon." But many were apathetic, and Major William H. Thomas wrote: "Mass Meeting today. Thayee and I listened awhile. Sun was hot, audience cold and speeches as far as we heard good in their way. . . . Allen's remarks abounded in poetic imagery."

The wildest rumors began to fly throughout the state—Smith would fight on, Allen had decided that surrender would be the best policy. William H. Tunnard reported that confusion "reigned everywhere among troops and citizens. . . . The men were gathered in groups everywhere, discussing the approaching surrender . . . the depth of feeling exhibited by compressed lips, pale faces, and blazing eyes, told a fearful story of how bitter was this hopeless surrender of the cause for which they had fought, toiled, suffered for long years." Many of the men, believing that the war was over and not wanting to officially surrender, simply walked or rode off and started for home; for they believed, as Winchester Hall wrote, that "they could not further serve the cause."

At Alexandria, Assistant Adjutant General David F. Boyd wrote to Colonel Amedee Bringier of the Seventh Louisiana Cavalry: "All is confusion and demoralization here, nothing like order or discipline remains. . . . There are but eighty-six men at the forts . . . in a word, colonel, the army is destroyed and we must look the matter square in the face and shape our actions (personally and officially) accordingly." In Shreveport, Kirby Smith prepared to move his headquarters to Houston, and Governor Allen went "about his duties as seemingly calm and self-controlled," Sarah Dorsey wrote, "as if he had been ignorant that a few days would end it all; that the sword of Damocles would soon break . . . and fall with mortal stroke upon his defenceless head."

The Last Days. On April 19, Federal General John Pope, commander of the military Division of Missouri, dispatched to Kirby Smith by Colonel John T. Sprague a communication proposing the same surrender terms Grant had given Lee. Arriving at the mouth of the Red River, Sprague refused to trust his letter to Confederate messengers or to meet with anyone less than the commanding general. He was conducted up the river toward Shreveport.

On the night of April 23, Confederate Lieutenant Charles W. Read, newly appointed captain of the heavily armed ram *Webb*, slowly nosed his ship out of the Red River into the Mississippi and began one of the most dramatic voyages in the history of the Confederate navy. He proceeded down the Mississippi, stopping at several places to cut telegraph lines, and reached New Orleans about noon of the twenty-fourth. Charging past the city and hotly pursued by several ships, he finally met the U.S.S. *Richmond* coming upriver and after a short fight ran the *Webb* ashore, fired, and burned her. Read and part of his crew escaped into the swamps.

The last month began, and time now moved with dramatic swiftess.

Colonel Sprague reached Shreveport on May 8 and immediately

conferred with Kirby Smith. General Pope had written that should Smith continue the hopeless struggle he would be "responsible for unnecessary bloodshed" and that "the duty of an officer is performed and his honor maintained when he has prolonged resistance until all hope of success has been lost."

Kirby Smith rejected Pope's proposals to surrender the Department, and invited the governors of Louisiana, Arkansas, Missouri, and Texas to meet at Marshall, Texas, to act upon "such important matters as are not embraced in my powers as commanding general." He also called a conference of the generals of the Department to meet at Marshall at the same time.

The representatives of the four states met on May 13, decided that the continuation of the war was impracticable, and prepared surrender terms which they would accept. Governor Allen was requested to "visit the United States authorities" to complete the "pacification of the Trans-Mississippi Department," but Colonel Sprague refused to give Allen conduct through the Federal lines, because, as he reported, "I did not feel at liberty to give a safeguard to the governor of a rebel State."

The generals decided that "a change of commanders was necessary," and General Buckner was selected to take command of the Confederate troops, which would be concentrated on the Brazos River. Should everything else fail, the remnants of the army of the Trans-Mississippi Department would then cross the Rio Grande "to take service with one or the other of the contending parties in Mexico and establish either an Empire or a Republic."

On May 15, Smith informed Colonel Sprague of the result of the governors' conference and emphasized that since his army was "not immediately threatened" he could not "submit to ignominious terms," but listed the terms of surrender acceptable to the Trans-Mississippi Department. Sprague then went to report to General Pope, while Smith prepared to move Departmental Headquarters to Houston, Texas.

By May 20 practically all of the Confederate forces in Louisiana had been paroled or discharged,* and David F. Boyd had written to Colonel Bringier that Generals Smith and Buckner were planning "to escape with a Corporal's Guard into Mexico." † The government

---

* Colonel Winchester Hall, in his account of the Twenty-sixth Louisiana Infantry, gives an example of the certificate of discharge: "This is to certify that Captain A. J. Moss has honorably served from the 10th March, 1862, to this date, in the Provisional Army Confederate States, and that this Brigade has from this day disbanded until further orders."

† Boyd was mistakenly referring to Missouri General Jo Shelby, who led about 1,000 ex-Confederates all the way to the City of Mexico, only to be rejected as a unified force by Emperor Maximilian. This dramatic, 2,000-mile march until recently was little known in American history, and even some modern Civil War historians have attributed its leadership to General Buckner. See Edwin Adams Davis, *Fallen Guidon; The Forgotten Saga of General Jo Shelby's Confederate Command, The Brigade That Never Surrendered, and Its Expedition to Mexico* (Santa Fe: Stagecoach Press, 1962).

stores at Shreveport were thrown open on May 21, and according to Louisiana historian J. Fair Hardin, "then began a scene which beggared description. Government stores . . . were seized, the streets filled with goods, official papers, etc., scattered everywhere. It was awful, terrible beyond portrayal." On May 23, General Joseph L. Brent arrived at Baton Rouge to arrange surrender terms with Federal General F. J. Herron. The next day, however, Confederate Generals Simon B. Buckner and Sterling Price arrived, and, picking up General Brent, proceeded to New Orleans to confer with General Canby.

On May 26, Buckner, acting in behalf of General Kirby Smith, signed the articles of surrender, which contained essentially the same terms as had Lee's surrender. Buckner insisted, however, that the document must be signed by General Smith before becoming official, so Federal General James J. Davis, with a copy, immediately left for Galveston on board the steamer *Fort Jackson*.

Kirby Smith meanwhile had arrived in Houston, where he found the Confederate forces in Texas so disintegrated that he was "a general without an army." He wrote Colonel Sprague that he was no longer in a position to surrender, for "the troops, with unexampled unanimity of action . . . have scattered to their homes. . . . The department is now open to occupation by your Government." In his last message to his soldiers he counseled them to "resume the occupations of peace. Yield obedience to the laws. . . . And may God, in his mercy, direct you aright, and heal the wounds of our distracted country." He went aboard the *Fort Jackson* at Galveston on June 2 and signed the document which surrendered the Trans-Mississippi Department and the widely scattered 18,000 troops still in uniform.

That same day, back in Shreveport, Governor Allen, who has been called "the greatest governor in Confederate history," turned the accounts of the state over to Colonel John M. Sandidge, issued his last message to the people of Louisiana, and departed for exile in Mexico. His parting message was an eloquent and moving one. He stated with firm resolve that "in this the darkest hour of my life, I do not come before you as an old man, broke down by storms of state, nor do I come to plead for mercy, at the hands of those whom I have fought for four long years. No, no, I come in the pride and vigor of manhood, unconquered, unsubdued. I have nothing to regret." He counseled the people to "Repair, improve, and plant. Go to work, with a hearty good-will. . . . Take the oath of allegiance. . . . If possible, forget the past. Look forward to the future. Act with candor and discretion, and you will live to bless him who in parting gives you this last advice."

A Federal order ending slavery in Louisiana reached Shreveport on June 3, and on that same day the ironclad *Missouri*, the last Confederate vessel on the Red River, was surrendered. Three days later the first detachment of temporary occupation troops under

General Herron reached the former Louisiana Confederate state capital and took possession of all remaining Confederate stores and of the Confederate and state records and archives. The twelve years of Federal military occupation of Louisiana officially began on June 20 with the arrival of the permanent occupation force of 5,000 Negro troops.

The South had lost its War for Independence. The last banner of the Stars and Bars would be lowered into the muddy waters of the Rio Grande at Eagle Pass, Texas, on July 4 by General Jo Shelby's volunteer Confederate Brigade on its way to the City of Mexico. In the years to come the words of Father Abram Ryan's "Conquered Banner" would seem peculiarly appropriate to the Southern heart:

> Furl that banner. True 'tis gory,
> Yet 'tis wreathed around with glory,
> And 'twill live in song and story,
> Tho its folds are in the dust:
> For its fame or brightest pages,
> Penned by poets and by sages,
> Shall go sounding down the ages,
> Furl its folds tho now we must.

The Long Trip Home. During those late spring and early summer days of 1865, Louisiana's Johnny Rebs came home, a bullet or two heavier or, because of a wound, illness, exposure, or poor and insufficient rations, a few pounds lighter than when the war began. Most of them walked back from Mississippi or Georgia or from Virginia and Appomattox, traveling slowly along the old Confederacy's country roads in pairs or threes, sometimes not speaking for miles, for there was not much to say. They were just tired and hungry, lonesome, defeat-saddened men, wishing that they were home.

Some of them carried the apathy of despair, faced burdens seemingly too heavy to be borne, turned their eyes from the desolation everywhere about them. Now that all was ended, they "sat patiently under the trees," as the rains beat upon them and the storm raged across their land. There was no more Confederate States of America, no Southern nation, no more armed resistance to the invader. Everywhere they looked there was "misery, poverty, graveyards." Many of the men envied their dead, those who had died upon the battlefields of the Confederacy.

Their driving force through four years of war had been a loyalty to the Cause, and pride—a reckless pride ready to flout a continent —for they knew that the finest honor and dignity that men have possessed have sprung from this ageless arrogance. But now they smelled of worn leather, and reeked of dirty clothing and stale body sweat, their shirts bleached beyond the butternut or even the gray and with the armpits white with salt brine, the gray hats battered and threadbare on the head, the sweatbands stinking when you eased up the brim. There were no flowers, no band music, no stirring speeches. There was only the dreariness and the stillness and the loneliness, and the final soul-inspiring knowledge to some of them that the men of this land had flung down their lives for a starred and barred flag which to them had been the symbol of something noble and lasting, something which would never be taken from them.

They perhaps recalled the farewell words of their commanders, as for example, those of Colonel J. S. Scott of the First Regiment, Louisiana Cavalry: "For nearly four years . . . you have borne the flag of your regiment with honor, with no stain upon its folds amid the smoke of battle." And Colonel Scott had continued that they should "maintain a consciousness of having faithfully rendered the service which Louisiana called upon you to perform," and of having faced "common suffering, common danger and common sacrifices."

In future years they would perhaps read the description of the last day of the Twenty-sixth and Twenty-eighth Louisiana Regiments, in camp near Mansfield, as written by Colonel Winchester Hall:

The 28th Louisiana gathered around the flag they had long followed with infinite credit. While the band played a dirge it was torn in pieces, and a piece given to each member as a memento. Not a word was spoken, but hardly an eye was not dimmed with a tear.

The 26th Louisiana gathered around its colors. Again a dirge was played by the band. The colors were taken down and torn in pieces. Silently, with heavy hearts and eyes that spoke more than words, each member took a piece. I broke the staff and burned it. . . .

As the tired veterans slowly moved along the roads, they saw gaunt chimneys, blackened stone or brick foundations, pieces of broken furniture or other wreckage lying among the weeds where once there had been gardens of shrubs and trees and flowers. And as they came around the bend of the bayou road, or topped the low, pine-covered hill, or watched the river or bayou waters rushing under the wheel of the steamer, they finally saw the village or town from which they had marched off to war. In most cases the place had changed little, except to age considerably, but sometimes, where the invader had been, as at Alexandria, Donaldsonville, Berwick City, Port Hudson, Milliken's Bend, Lake Providence, New Carthage, Bruinsburg, Ponchatoula, and other places, there just was not much left but blackened, rain-washed ruins.

Even after he had been home for a spell and had rested and filled out some, a man would fall silent at times and just stare off into space, and then the wife might remark that her husband was "off to war again, where I can't follow and be with him." But this reclusive lonesomeness would be a part of him for the rest of his life.

The heroic years of the Johnny Rebs of Louisiana had ended. They had fought as valiantly for the independence of the Confederate States of America as their forefathers had fought for the independence of the old Union—but they had lost. The cause for which they had charged into the foreground of many a terrible, pitiless battle had perished by the sword. Now there was a Dead Sea behind them. Bury that dead and bitter past where it belonged, beneath the ashes of a fallen Confederacy and a fallen Cause. There was today to think of—and tomorrow, and tomorrow.

X

Federal Occupation and Wartime "Reconstruction"

General Benjamin F. Butler. A week after the Federal occupation of New Orleans began, the "Wife of a Southern Planter" wrote the commanding general that "when our gallant Beauregard comes to deliver us . . . we shall see with intense joy the noble Picayune Butler flying . . . in finished *Bull Run* or *Bethel* style, with all the Yankee rabble infesting our city at his heels." No one was ever more incorrect, for the occupying army remained in New Orleans and in Louisiana for nearly fifteen years.

General Butler established his headquarters at the St. Charles Hotel in the late afternoon of May 1, 1862, while a military band played "The Star-Spangled Banner," "Yankee Doodle," and other stirring United States musical compositions to drown out the jeers, catcalls, and cheers for Jefferson Davis and the Confederacy emanating from a large crowd of citizens. He conferred that evening with Mayor John T. Monroe, the City Council, and Pierre Soule, informing the Southerners that he had come to rescue the city from "the hand of a foreign government" and from "domestic insurrection." In his first proclamation he listed the regulations for governing the city and insisted that he had come "to restore order out of chaos and the government of laws in place of the passions of men." It was his hope, he concluded, "to exercise this government mildly," that it should "not be rigorously and firmly administered."

The forty-four-year-old Federal general was a successful lawyer with a large personal fortune and was a Democratic party leader of growing national stature, who had served in the Massachusetts Legislature and was especially popular with labor because of his espousal of a ten-hour day. He had voted for the nomination of Jefferson Davis at the deadlocked Charleston Democratic Convention of 1860 and had subsequently supported Southern Democrat presidential candidate John C. Breckinridge.

A stout, somewhat shapeless man, with a fair complexion, frequently changed to florid by anger or excitement, Butler had bright but squinting eyes, one of them so out of focus that his soldiers called him "Old Cock-eye." He had "a large half-bald head, from the back of which thin, grey hair fell over his ears," heavy features, and a "highkeyed, penetrating, tranquil drawl which makes the men titter." According to one contemporary, his arms and legs looked "as if made for somebody else, and hastily glued to him by mistake." He had little grace or fluency of speech but was firm, imposing, solid. He was short of temper, loved controversy, and had a brilliant intellect. Although certainly no pretender and no hypocrite, he was pompous and tactless. He had social charm when he wished to exert it, but possessed a coarseness well illustrated by his remark when a group of New Orleans women turned their backs to him—they knew which end of them looked best. He was generally popular with his soldiers, perhaps because they enjoyed making fun of his high-pitched voice and his somewhat grotesque actions; one of them wrote that he "tumbles all to pieces with distress. His body jerks forward; his elbows flap up and down like wings; he seems to trot several feet ahead of his horse; he arrives at the scene of confusion with a face of anguish."

Problems of "Occupied" City Administration and Relief. Butler suspended the city government, forbade all assemblages of persons in the streets, ordered all Confederates to surrender their flags, "their arms, equipments, and munitions of war," and decreed that the American flag "must be treated with the utmost deference and respect." He closed "all public houses, coffee houses, and drinking saloons" until such time as they might be licensed by the Provost Marshal, but permitted the continued circulation of Confederate bank notes. All persons were to be given the opportunity to "renew their oath of allegiance" to the United States and thereafter to hold property subject to American laws. Other general regulations provided for the preservation of order and the replacing of Confederate with United States government.

Butler quickly restored order in a city which had been in a state of constant rioting for several days. Patrols moved along their patterned routes on a twenty-four-hour schedule. Soldiers were quickly brought under tight discipline—when one group of them plundered a number of houses, four men were promptly hanged. Within a week the streets were quiet.

Thousands of people were out of work and destitute and hundreds had been on direct relief for over a year, for economic depression had hit with full force after the establishment of the Federal naval blockade in 1861. Butler immediately fixed food prices in order to curb profiteering (the price of flour had risen to $14.00 a barrel), ordered emergency rations to be shipped through army channels to New Orleans, and levied special taxes to feed and care for the poor. By October, 1862, he reported that he was feeding 10,000 families a month at a cost of $70,000, spending $2,000 for the support of five orphanages, and $5,000 for Charity Hospital, and that during one typical week 34,200 people had received "more

84

than 23,000 pounds of pork, 48,000 pounds of beef, and 92,000 loaves of bread."

He set hundreds of unemployed men to cleaning streets, repairing wharves, enlarging drainage ditches and canals, flushing filthy gutters, repairing levees, and filling in sections of the river front with *batture* sand. Even bitter critic Marion Southwood was impressed and wrote that Butler was "the best scavenger we have ever had." He enforced quarantine and fumigation regulations. A few years after the war a writer in the New Orleans *Journal of Medicine* admitted that Butler's regime had been characterized by three exceptional facts: the absence of epidemics, a better quarantine than the civil authorities had ever imposed, and the enforcement of sanitary regulations by an efficient police.

But economic prosperity returned slowly to the Crescent City, even though the port was opened to world trade in June and the prices of most commodities were such that traders with either capital or credit could not avoid making money—sugar, for example, sold for three cents a pound in New Orleans and for six cents in New York; turpentine was $3.00 a barrel in New Orleans and $38.00 in New York; other commodities were priced in like proportion. It must be remembered, however, that only those who took the oath of allegiance were cleared for business activity; as James Parton wrote: "For Union men there were offices, employments, privileges, favors, honors, everything which a government can bestow. For rebels there was mere protection against personal violence—mere toleration of their presence; and that only so long as they remained perfectly submissive and quiescent." Visiting English merchant W. C. Corsan wrote that in the fall of 1862 New Orleans businessmen had little to do except curse "the common foe," and that the city "exceeded in dulness any little country-town I ever saw the day after market-day."

It was not until the reopening of the St. Louis, Cincinnati, Louisville, and Pittsburgh trade in the fall of 1863 that industry and business began to show signs of improvement.

Problems of Keeping Order. The commander of the occupying Federal forces was in a trying position. He was the military commandant of the largest and most complex city in the South, one of the proudest and most loyal cities of the Confederacy, a city "of a hundred and fifty thousand inhabitants, all hostile, bitter, defiant, explosive." He had not counted on cordiality from a people "smarting with the humiliation of defeat," but he hardly expected the treatment he and his men immediately received from the civilian population, which did everything possible to ridicule, insult, and annoy the soldiers of the occupying army. The women of the upper classes were generally politely insulting, for example refusing to sit with Federal soldiers in a horsecar or in a church pew; many of the lower classes screamed crude epithets and filthy abuse and acted out studied, exaggerated insults whenever a blue uniform appeared, spit on officers and enlisted men, and dumped slops on unsuspecting heads from upper windows and balconies. The *Daily Picayune* on May 9, 1862, wrote of the "shameless conduct" of the women of the city, the "shocking nuisance" of their street behavior, and demanded their arrest "whether arrayed in fine clothes or in rags," but newspaper comments had no effect.

On May 15, Butler issued General Order No. 28, which stated that as the officers and soldiers of the United States Army had been subject to the repeated insults of the women of New Orleans, "in return for the most scrupulous noninterference and courtesy on our part, it is ordered that hereafter when any female shall, by word, gesture, or movement, insult or show contempt for any officer or soldier of the United States, she shall be regarded and held liable to be treated as a woman of the town plying her vocation." This meant that a woman, upon formal complaint, might be arrested, held overnight in the city jail, brought before a magistrate the next morning, and if found guilty, fined $5.00.

Mayor Monroe and Governor Moore immediately protested, and soon protests were received from over the entire world. "Probably no other action by an American military commander," as Herbert Asbury wrote, "ever aroused such a worldwide storm of resentment and indignation." Southerners believed that the order gave Federal troops permission to insult the women of New Orleans and so advertised the order, and the world answered by condemning Butler as few men have ever been condemned. The editor of the La Crosse (Wisconsin) *Democrat* called him "hell's blackest imp; Apollyon's twin brother; the Grand High-priest of Pandaemonium; the unclean, perjured, false-hearted product of Massachusetts civilization . . . the dirtiest knave God ever gave breath to; total depravity personified; that baggy-faced fruit of perdition, Beast Butler!" A Confederate soldier wrote the following acrostic:

> B eastly by instinct, a tyrant and sot,
> U gly and venemous—on mankind a blot—
> T hief, liar, and scoundrel, in highest degree,
> L et Yankeedom boast of such heroes as thee!
> E very woman and child will for ages to come
> R emember thee, monster—vilest of scum!

But whatever the criticism, the order had the desired effect, and Butler later wrote that "no woman has either insulted or annoyed" a Federal soldier and no soldier has made "a false move towards any respectable woman." New Orleans quieted down.

Three weeks later, on June 5, Butler issued Special Order No. 70, approving the execution of forty-one-year-old William B. Mumford, who had been tried and convicted by a military commission for treason and the "overt act thereof . . . for the purpose of inciting other evil-minded persons to further resistance" against the United States by pulling down the American flag from the United

States Mint, two days before the formal occupation of the city. Tremendous pressure was brought to bear on Butler to spare Mumford, including personal pleas by Mayor Monroe and noted citizen Dr. William Newton Mercer, but the sentence was carried out. Mumford immediately became a hero to the people of New Orleans, Louisiana, and the South, and Butler his murderer.

A week later the General ordered five members of a seven-man, Federal-soldier group who had robbed nearly a score of private homes to be hanged, the last executions during the entire period of Butler's regime. From this time on, according to Butler, there were no burglaries, no incendiary fires, no assaults with intent to kill, only petty larcenies and other such minor crimes. But there was a great deal of friction between Butler and Mayor Monroe, who protested General Order No. 28 so vehemently that Butler suspended him "from the exercise of any functions" and sent him to Fort Jackson. Schools, churches, newspapers, banks, and all city agencies were soon placed under Federal authority.

Problem of the Newly Freed Slaves. The slave Negro was perhaps the greatest single problem facing Federal civil and military officials in occupied Louisiana. Many slaves were ordered off or forcibly carried from the plantations by detachments of Federal troops; others deserted the plantations, attached themselves to army units, crowded into New Orleans and other towns, or simply began to wander aimlessly about the countryside. Within a short time after the occupation of New Orleans it was estimated that over 10,000 ex-slaves were living "from hand-to-mouth" in and about the city. Negro crime in some sections could not be controlled, for marching groups with flags and drums, shouting, "Abe Lincoln and Freedom," destroyed property, looted plantations, attacked persons, and committed robberies and murders in isolated areas. But many of them returned to their masters "weary and footsore and eager to get home."

The problem of Negro vagrants became so acute that in August, 1862, General Butler authorized their enlistments in the Federal army. Within four months three regiments of "Louisiana Native Guards" and one regiment of heavy artillery had been enlisted from the New Orleans area. But the colored troops caused a great deal of trouble. It was difficult to get white officers to command them, and frequently low-class white officers abused their men. Officers reported that "something was always out of joint" with Negro troops, and Lawrence Van Alstyne wrote that one Negro soldier "whom I had taken extra pains to educate, I found taking his gun apart to see how it was made. Another had his shoes and stockings off and was walking his beat with bare feet. Another had taken off his accoutrements and piled them up at the end of his beat and was strutting back and forth with folded arms." General Henry W. Halleck wrote that they could be best "used with advantage as laborers, teamsters, cooks, &c," and Abolitionist Senator James

Lane of Kansas admitted that "no man in his sober senses will say their services are worth much."

In spite of all of the problems connected with the use of colored troops, however, a few over 24,000 were enlisted in Louisiana, more than in any other state of the South, and more than the total number in the combined states of Alabama, Arkansas, Florida, Georgia, and North and South Carolina.

Confiscating and "Butlerizing." Shortly after Federal Colonel A. J. H. Duganne arrived in New Orleans, he wrote: "I fancy this Crescent City may, ere long, be a paradise for paymasters who, on majors' stipend, shall get rich betimes; and that quartermasters here, on captains' pay, shall win their Golden Fleeces easier than Jason did." The "plucking" of the "Louisiana bird of paradise" had already begun, and would continue until the restoration of Home Rule in the spring of 1877.

On June 10, 1862, Butler issued General Order No. 41, which stated that all former citizens of the United States who wished "any favor, protection, privilege, passport" or any benefit "except protection from personal violence" must take the oath of allegiance to the United States. During the rest of the summer, however, only a small percentage of New Orleanians and Louisianians living in occupied territory took the oath. Butler, therefore, ordered the Federal Confiscation Act of July 17 put into effect on September 23. There was a rush of oath taking, and nearly 70,000 persons had affixed their names to the legal forms by the last of October. Of course, everyone well understood, as Butler biographer James Parton wrote, that the "mere form of words" was "not binding upon the consciences" of the people of New Orleans and southeast Louisiana. But the property of those who signed the oath was saved; that of persons away from their homes or in Confederate military service or who refused to sign was promptly seized and sold at auction.

While Federal common soldiers were held on tight rein, officers and Northern civilians who flocked like locusts to New Orleans acquired confiscated property of all types, for personal use or for speculation, at Federal auctions at greatly reduced prices, sometimes only 10 per cent of the value of the item, by the simple process of not bidding against each other, and engaged in any type of endeavor which would yield a profit. In all probability Butler himself acquired no property in this manner, but his brother, "Colonel" A. J. Butler, and numerous others reputedly made fortunes by various forms of extralegal and illegal practices. The word "Butlerize," meaning to steal, came into common use; British traveler David Macrae on several occasions heard people speak of having had possessions "Butlerized." Butler was criticized by Secretary of the Treasury Salmon P. Chase for tolerating the corrupt activities of his friends and his brother, and Quaker temperance reformer General Neal Dow was openly twitted about his "penchant" for "rebel" furniture.

The case of George S. Denison, Collector of United States Customs, Special Agent of the Treasury Department, and holder of other Federal positions in New Orleans from May, 1862, until June, 1865, is an excellent example of the financial activities of the civilian-military officer group. Denison reached New Orleans in early June, and soon sent home his first shipment of "rebel curiosities." Shortly afterwards, he wrote his mother: "Whenever I send anything home please say nothing about it. . . . I don't want . . . the public to know of, nor meddle with my business." During the following three years he sent a wide variety of items home, including a "fine Iron Cannon (6 pounder) which the rebels threw in the river" and about which he wrote his uncle: "Wasn't it rather absurd for me to send home that big Cannon?" He speculated in corn, cotton, and sugar, was a partner in the owning and operation of several large plantations, was an organizing partner of a bank ("It is a big thing."), and acquired other business interests not identified in his letters.

General Butler was replaced on December 16, 1862, by "handsome and dapper" General Nathaniel P. Banks, who was reputed to be the best Federal general "selected from civil life," for he had been a state legislator, member of Congress, Speaker of the House of Representatives, and Governor of Massachusetts. General Butler left New Orleans on December 24, and one New Orleanian reported: "There was not one hurrah, not one sympathizing cry went up for him from the vast crowd which went to see him off—a silent rebuke. I wonder if he felt it!"

Although Banks eased regulations, the confiscation of property in Federal occupied areas continued until the end of the war. Most New Orleanians, naturally, never became reconciled to Federal occupation, and when on one occasion someone remarked to General Banks that New Orleans was a Union city, he replied: "A Union city? I could carry every Union man in it on a hand-car."

But it should be strongly emphasized that the confiscation of Confederate property in Louisiana was in complete conformance with the Federal Confiscation Act, and while Louisiana historians have unanimously castigated Butler, there is no evidence that he at any time went beyond the law. The Congress and the President of the United States should receive the blame, not the commanding general at New Orleans. At no time during Butler's regime was there the completely unrestrained looting and destruction of property later permitted by General Banks in the Teche Country and in the Red River Valley and by General U. S. Grant in northeast Louisiana. Nevertheless, to many Southerners he has remained "Silver Spoon" Butler, to others less restrained, the "hideous cross-eyed beast."

Wartime "Reconstruction" of Occupied Louisiana. From May 1, 1862, until the end of the war two governments operated in Louisiana, that of the United States civil-military authorities in the eastern and southeastern areas occupied by Federal troops, and the Confederate government of Thomas Overton Moore and Henry Watkins Allen.

Lincoln hoped to reconstruct Louisiana for readmission into the old Union at the same time war was being waged against the other states of the South. He hoped, and apparently expected, that many Louisianians would give him their support. Writing to New Yorker August Belmont, on July 31, 1863, Lincoln said: "Broken eggs cannot be mended; but Louisiana has nothing to do now but take her place in the Union as it was, barring the already broken eggs. The sooner she does so, the smaller will be the amount of that which will be past mending."

Municipal and state courts began functioning again in New Orleans shortly after its occupation, and in the last of December, 1862, the "United States Provisional Court for the State of Louisiana," one of the most unusual legal bodies in American history, was opened. Michael Hahn and Benjamin F. Flanders were elected to Congress from the First and Second Districts in early December and were admitted to Congress, but served only until March 4, 1863. A small Conservative group held an election in St. Bernard and Plaquemines parishes in November, 1863, and elected Joshua Baker, Thomas Cottman, and A. P. Field to Congress and John L. Riddell to the governorship, but the men were not permitted to take their offices. Louisiana Representatives or Senators were not admitted to Congress until after the war.

In middle January, 1864, General Banks, as Military Commander of Louisiana, proclaimed that on February 22 would be held an election for state officials, in which loyal citizens and ex-Confederates who had taken the oath of allegiance could vote. Two political parties were organized, the Conservative party, generally composed of old-line Southern Democrats, and the Free State party, made up of a few Republicans, opponents of secession, and those citizens who had accepted Lincoln's plan of government. Michael Hahn was "elected" governor and J. Madison Wells lieutenant governor by the Free State group, even though of the total of only 11,000 votes cast, nearly 1,000 had been cast by Federal troops stationed in Louisiana and at Fort Barrancas, Florida. Hahn was inaugurated at the City Hall in New Orleans on March 4, 1864, a Federal-army-supported governor of less than half the state, without a legally elected legislature, and unable to govern under the state constitution.

Immediately after Hahn's inauguration, Banks ordered an election of delegates to a convention to revise the state Constitution of 1852. The convention, in no sense a representative body, met for seventy-eight days during the early summer of 1864 (during which period it spent $120.78 a day for liquors, cigars, and other sundry items and ran up a total cost of $364,000) and on July 23 adopted a new constitution which abolished slavery, extended suffrage to Negroes who had served in the Federal army, who owned taxable property, or who showed intellectual fitness; broadened the powers of the Legislature; and extended public education. The constitution, as Roger Shugg has written, was "an extraordinary document which contained reforms and innovations of great social import," but while it remedied many farmer and laborer grievances, some of its innovations were revolutionary and ahead of the times.

The constitution was adopted, and members of the Legislature and Representatives to Congress elected September 5, 1864. Five Representatives and two Senators went to Washington to represent Louisiana at the next session of Congress, but were not admitted to membership. Hahn served as Governor of "occupied" Louisiana until March, 1865, when he resigned after his election by the Legislature to the United States Senate, and was succeeded by Lieutenant Governor J. Madison Wells. He continued as Governor until removed by General William T. Sherman during the summer of 1867.

XI

State and Local Government During Wartime

Wartime Governors. Confederate Louisiana had two governors during the War for Southern Independence, Thomas Overton Moore, North Carolina–born planter of Rapides Parish, and Henry Watkins Allen, Virginia-born lawyer-planter of West Baton Rouge Parish. They were able, conscientious men, and while Allen was the abler of the two, Moore has never been given just recognition for his four years of service.

During his first year in office, Moore directed the mobilization of Louisiana's manpower and economic resources for war, constantly pleading with the Confederate States government for additional much-needed support. With the capture of New Orleans, he lost control of the southeastern parishes, and with the fall of Port Hudson and Vicksburg lost the eastern one third of the state. His luster as a war governor was somewhat dimmed by his migration in the fall of 1864 with a contingent of slaves to Crockett, Texas, preparatory to settling permanently in Mexico. He remained in Texas until the war's end, when he traveled to Mexico and then to Cuba. After receiving his parole from President Andrew Johnson in November, 1865, he returned to Rapides Parish, to live at his "Emfield" plantation home until his death in 1876.

After a Missouri boyhood, Henry Watkins Allen established a school at Grand Gulf, Mississippi, in 1842. He lived for a time in the Republic of Texas, returned to Mississippi, married, served a term in the lower house of the Mississippi Legislature, became a Louisiana planter, took advanced law courses at Harvard University, traveled in Europe (which resulted in the publication of *The Travels of a Sugar Planter*), and was a member of the Louisiana House of Representatives when secession came. He was commissioned a colonel in the Fourth Louisiana Infantry, was wounded at Shiloh and at the Battle of Baton Rouge, and in September, 1863, was commissioned brigadier general by President Jefferson Davis. Robert Patrick wrote that when Allen left his old command "he made us a speech, and shook hands and bade farewell to his old Regiment. It was quite affecting and there was scarcely a dry eye in the Regiment. He was loved by the men, for he was always their friend, and a braver man never lived. . . ."

The gubernatorial election of 1863 was unusual in that both Allen and his principal opponent, Colonel Leroy Stafford of Rapides Parish, were in the army; neither, therefore, waged an active campaign in the nineteen parishes in possession of the Confederate state government. Allen was elected by a landslide vote of 7,401 to 872 for Stafford; even the Federal-controlled New Orleans *Era* admitted that he "is one of the best fighting-men the rebels have in the Southwest, and is quite popular with the rank and file."

Allen took office at Shreveport on January 25, 1864, and shortly afterwards toured Confederate Louisiana, giving much "strength" to the people "by his kindly sympathy and ardent words." He made an enviable record during his sixteen-month period as governor and at the end of the war went into exile in Mexico, where he edited the English-language City of Mexico *Mexican Times* until his death in 1866.*

Capitals of the State During Wartime. The seat of state government at the beginning of the war was Baton Rouge where the new capitol, overlooking the Mississippi at the foot of Third Street, had been completed in 1850. After the capture of New Orleans, the capital was moved temporarily to Opelousas, described by Northern traveler Frederick Law Olmsted as "a pleasant village, with shaded streets, and many substantial mansions, and pretty cottages." Executive offices were leased in the Lacombe Hotel on Court Street opposite the courthouse square, and rooms in the courthouse and in nearby buildings were made available for state-government use. The Legislature met at Opelousas in its December, 1862–January, 1863 session, during which an act was passed moving the capital to Shreveport in Caddo Parish for the remainder of the war.

In the late spring of 1863 the seat of government was moved to Shreveport, which J. W. Dorr of the New Orleans *Crescent* called "the commercial emporium of Northwestern Louisiana, a flourishing young city." The new $19,000 courthouse became the state capitol, while the offices of the Governor, according to historian J. Fair Hardin, were located "in an old frame building . . . on the north side of Texas Street at Nos. 724–726, adjoining Renfro's Drug Store."

Louisiana in the Confederacy. The six delegates to the Montgomery Convention, which set up the government of the Confederate States of America, have been characterized as "among the most eminent citizens of Louisiana, men of high character and deeply interested in the state's prosperity." They represented the state in the Confederate Congress until replaced by regularly elected congressional members in February, 1862.

The first election for Louisiana's members of the Confederate

* The only complete file of Allen's newspaper is in the Library of Louisiana State University.

House of Representatives was held on November 4, 1861, and Lucien J. Dupre, Charles M. Conrad (former United States Senator and Secretary of War), Duncan F. Kenner (long-time state Whig party leader), Henry Marshall, John Perkins, Jr., and Charles Villere were elected. On November 28, the Legislature elected Edward Sparrow of Concordia Parish and T. J. Semmes of Orleans Parish to represent the state in the Confederate Senate. The two Senators and five of the Representatives served throughout the period of the Confederacy. Representative Henry Marshall did not run for re-election and was succeeded by Colonel Benjamin L. Hodge, of Caddo Parish, who died in August, 1864; Hodge was followed by Henry Gray, also of Caddo Parish, through a special election the following October.

Several Louisianians occupied posts of distinction in or under the Confederate government. Judah P. Benjamin, born on the West Indian island of St. Croix, a noted jurist and United States Senator (1852–61), served successively as Confederate Attorney-General, Secretary of War, and finally as Secretary of State, in which capacity he became known as the "brains of the Confederacy." Former United States Senator John Slidell represented the Confederate government in France; Pierre A. Rost was a member of the Confederacy's first European mission and later served in Spain; A. B. Roman was one of the three Confederate peace commissioners who in 1861 attempted to negotiate a peaceful secession of the Southern states. Duncan F. Kenner was sent to Europe as a special Confederate Minister Plenipotentiary early in 1865, after having been Chairman of the Committee on Ways and Means in the House of Representatives.

The government of the Confederate States of America was, in many respects, a complete paradox to the governmental heritage of the American people. The people of the South, intense believers in the doctrine of state rights, adopted a constitution withholding from their central government practically all the fundamental powers of government. Yet the Richmond government rapidly became a despotism, in many respects wielding absolute power over the Southern states and their citizens. One contemporary wrote: "It tolerated no questioning, brooked no resistance, listened to no remonstrance." But Louisiana and the other Southern states, knowing that the central government of the Confederacy could be destroyed at any time and that the first objective of the new nation was to win independence from the United States, accepted constant encroachment upon personal and state rights during the four years of the government's existence.

Problems of State Government. The crisis over the nature of the American Union was rushing rapidly toward a climax when Governor Moore took office in January, 1860; within a little over a year Louisiana had seceded and had joined the new Southern republic. The war began three months later. The two war governors of Louisiana, therefore, had to direct the ordinary functions of state government while at the same time providing for the military needs of a state either threatened with or actually invaded by enemy forces.

The state government faced numerous wartime problems. The Legislature passed civil and criminal laws, but the presence of Federal armies made enforcement impossible in areas they controlled and materially added to the routine difficulties of law enforcement in the Confederate sections. Substitutes had to be found for state and local officials who had joined the armed forces. Governmental and legal records were captured or destroyed, making court trials difficult and seriously affecting land titles, mortgages, contracts, and other legal transactions. The case of Harp *v.* Kenner in Ascension Parish is an excellent example: It concerned the payment of a note, and the man who executed the note was killed, one of the endorsers was in the Confederate Congress while another was in Lee's army in Virginia, the holder of the note was a prisoner of war in the North, the maker of the note was dead, and finally, the parish recorder's office had been burned by Federal troops in October, 1862.

Problems of wartime finance and taxation were, indeed, insurmountable; only a complete revolution in these phases of government would have fundamentally aided in their solution. At the beginning of 1861, the state was in sound financial condition, with total liabilities of only slightly more than $10,000,000 and a favorable balance of receipts over expenditures for the preceding year of $155,000. The banks were strong and those in New Orleans held over $17,500,000 in specie and had more than $22,750,000 on deposit; but specie payments were suspended in the fall of 1861, and soon Confederate, state, and parish paper money began to depreciate in value. The payment of taxes was suspended from January, 1862, until February, 1865, when a legislative act provided that back taxes for the years 1860, 1861, and 1864 would be forgiven if the 1862 and 1863 taxes were paid in full. With very little revenue being received, the state had to issue treasury notes and to sell bonds, but they also soon depreciated in value.

Shortly after taking office in 1864, Governor Allen established state stores where the depreciated money would be accepted at face value. The new plan worked so well that a modern historian has written that Allen "was the single great administrator produced by the Confederacy. His success in Louisiana indicates that he might have changed history . . . if his talents could have been utilized by the Confederate government." But throughout the war there was much ordinary bartering and the payment of taxes "in kind" with corn, potatoes, bacon, cotton, and other products; as taxes in kind did not bring in enough supplies, the government was forced to "impress" goods needed for military purposes.

During the entire course of the war, particularly during Allen's administration, state officials gave much attention to the establishment of factories to produce the necessities of everyday living or of war, and to the building of depots to distribute these items. Basic war needs included cannon, small arms, ammunition, supply vehicles, tents, uniforms and other types of clothing, a wide variety of food supplies, medicines, hospital equipment, and other goods necessary to support fighting men whether in the field or in camp. Civilian needs included all the necessities of life which had not been produced within the state prior to the war and which now could not be imported from other Southern states, the United States, or foreign countries. The Confederate government at Richmond was never able to give Louisiana much assistance in furnishing these civilian and military needs.

The most important factories included foundries, armories, powder plants, tanneries, cotton-cloth manufactories, packing houses for the production of salt pork and salt beef, shoe factories, harness shops, and mills for grinding flour and corn meal. Mills were established in St. Mary Parish, in Caddo, and in other northern parishes; evaporation salt works were built in several parishes including Bienville, Bossier, and Winn; slaughterhouses for beef and hogs were opened in northern and western towns. While large amounts of beef, pork, meal, flour, salt, cotton cloth, and other goods for use east of the Mississippi were produced, the constant patrolling of the Mississippi after the fall of Vicksburg and Port Hudson seriously affected distribution, in spite of a considerable amount of smuggling across the river in small, dark-painted, flat-bottomed, oar-propelled boats.

Keeping the Ranks Filled. Louisiana had rapidly mobilized her military strength in 1861. United States military property was occupied, the Military Board organized military districts, male citizens were made subject to militia duty, supplies were deposited in government warehouses, thousands of patriotic men joined the military service, and assistance to soldiers and their families was organized on a state-wide basis.

The militia system was reorganized by the Legislature early in 1862. State officials, legislators, judges, parish officials, ministers, physicians, mayors of towns, and a few other groups were exempted from military service. Enlistment was for ninety days, although the Governor might in an unusual emergency extend the service period an additional six months. The Governor appointed all militia officers above the rank of captain with the exception of the major general, who was elected by the Legislature. Early in 1863 new military regulations, repealing those of the preceding year, authorized the Governor to "raise an Army" for the defense of the state, to be called the "Army for the State of Louisiana." To be used within the state only, it would be composed of men enlisted for twelve months, and total enlistments would not exceed 20,000. Each soldier would receive a bounty payment of $50.00 and a grant of eighty acres of land at the end of the war. Additional militia laws were later passed by the Legislature, some of which were considered harsh and unfair to the nonslaveholding, poorer classes of society.

In his first message to the Legislature, Allen recommended that the Governor be authorized to organize a State Guard and that all white men between the ages of fifteen and fifty-five not in some branch of Confederate military service be enrolled, armed, and equipped for short-term duty of not more than "sixty days at a time" within the state. These men would not be subject to field service except to check "the raids and incursions of the enemy." The authorization was granted, and some of the newly formed units fought at Mansfield and Pleasant Hill. A new militia act was signed by Governor Allen in February, 1864, but two months later all Southern state militias were removed from state control and were incorporated into the reserve corps of the Army of the Confederate States.

But the various militia and conscription acts did not meet the needs of Louisiana and of the Confederacy. Officials of the State Conscript Bureau became increasingly vigilant as the months passed, systematically checked census and tax rolls, and set up permanent or temporary conscription offices in every parish. Many soldiers and prospective soldiers hired men who were exempt from military service to take their places in the ranks. Edwin H. Fay, for example, had much to say on this subject in his letters to his wife. In May, 1862, he wrote that "I will give my horse, bridle and saddle and $400 per year as long as the war lasts to any healthy man to take my place. If your Father can find such a man send him on to me by all means." Substitutes were hired until the practice was stopped by the Confederate government near the end of 1862.

Draft-Dodgers, "Fair-Weather" Patriots, Spies, and Jayhawkers. The slow decline of Confederate Louisiana began with the loss of Port Hudson and Vicksburg in July, 1863. Until then the great majority of the people had loyally supported the state, the Confederacy, and the war. While there had been a good deal of illicit trading with the enemy; a fair amount of tax evasion and refusal to accept Confederate currency; some theft of military equipment and supplies; some giving of information to the enemy, desertion and stirring up of discontent; and actual plundering and burning in isolated areas by jayhawkers, these "fair-weather-patriot" or treasonable practices had not caused the state government very much concern. Now they became serious.

Draft-dodgers and deserters took to the swamps and hills in large enough numbers to actually impair the efficiency of the military forces. A modern authority has stated that several areas of northern Louisiana "became infested with deserters, draft-dodgers, and bands of jayhawkers," and that deserters were "especially numerous in Catahoula and along the Pearl River in the Florida parishes." Draft-dodgers were tried by civil courts, deserters by courts-martial; jayhawkers were in most cases condemned without trial and often were shot without the courtesy of the customary blindfold.

A small number of Louisianians actually spied for the enemy, either for laudable reasons of loyalty to the Old Republic or for economic gain. These people secured details on numbers and equipment of troops located at specific points, reported troop movements, diagrammed fortifications, located hidden supplies and depots of cotton and other products, checked gunboat activities on rivers and bayous, and performed other services. Governor Moore admitted that spies and salaried informers were constant visitors to areas not under complete Federal occupation. In May, 1864, for example, Federal General E. R. S. Canby, needing information on the railroad from Vicksburg to Monroe and on the projected line to Shreveport, ordered spies into the area who "should be intelligent inhabitants of the country."

Beginning with the late summer of 1863, state and local government officials were plagued in several sections of the state by the activities of organized bands of jayhawkers who plundered the countryside, burned houses and other buildings, sometimes killed civilians who opposed them or who were stanch Confederates, gave considerable aid to the Federals, and in St. Mary Parish incited a slave uprising. These groups were particularly active in the Atakapas country of southwest Louisiana, in Ascension and Livingston parishes, in Catahoula, Winn, and Caldwell parishes, and in several other smaller sections of North and Central Louisiana. A few of the leaders were rewarded with commissions in the Federal army or with political appointments either during the war or afterwards by the Radical state government.

Despite a few successful expeditions against these groups, they operated in both Confederate and Federal-occupied sections of Louisiana until the end of the war. At one time General Taylor admitted that he did not have enough cavalry to adequately destroy or scatter them. Not infrequently Confederate officers home on leave would organize jayhawk-hunting posses. On one occasion General St. John R. Liddell of Catahoula Parish brought a hundred of his soldiers home with him and "they rounded up some of the 'Jayhawkers' in the Catahoula hills and swamps, and lined them up before a firing squad. Only one man lived to tell it." Companies of Patrols, Home Guards, and Partisan Rangers were organized to defend Louisianians living within the Confederate lines from their own people; two of the most noted companies of Rangers, for example, operated in Rapides Parish and Central Louisiana and were led by David C. Paul and James A. McWaters.

Local and Parish Problems. Police juries, town councils, and other local officials faced numerous extraordinary as well as routine responsibilities during the war years. While many of their records were destroyed by Federal soldiers, fire, or careless handling by

98

officials of postwar or more modern times, enough remain to reveal many of the everyday problems of local government during the harrowing days of the 1860's. Local governmental officials paid bounties to enlistees, purchased equipment and supplies for newly organized military companies, furnished relief to needy families, repaired roads, ferries, levees, and bridges, attempted to maintain order, levied and collected taxes, kept the soldier ranks filled, and otherwise executed the responsibilities of their offices.

In Avoyelles Parish in 1861, for example, after having appropriated money for education and roads and a new jail, the police jurors gave funds to Captain Boone's company, Captain Johnson's company, and to Captain Cannon of the "Creole Chargers," levied taxes, continued road patrols, ordered levees repaired, and contracted for a "plank fence built around the new jail." They authorized the payment of $40.00 to each infantryman, $75.00 to each cavalryman, and $5.00 per month to each "wife or mother of a soldier in need." Two years later, the jury spent $20,320 for soldier family relief and in September, 1864, expended $40,630 for the same purpose.

At the July, 1861, meeting of the Concordia Parish Police Jury, the members appropriated $10,000 "for the purpose of arming and equipping such military corps as may be raised in this parish," voted $200 per year to Mrs. Mary White, "whose son and son-in-law are in Virginia fighting the battles of our country," and resolved "that should the war not be terminated by our October meeting, that we favor assessing at that time a war tax of $50,000.00." At the October meeting, the jury appropriated more than $14,000 to military companies, including "$2005.68 for underclothing for 'Concordia Rifles,'" thanked "the Ladies Confederate Sewing Society of Natchez for their valuable aid," levied new taxes, and authorized the parish tax collector to accept Confederate Treasury and Louisiana Bank notes in payment of taxes.

XII

Economy in a War-torn State

General Economic Conditions. After the end of the war, a traveler in the Red River Valley wrote that the plantations, towns, and villages of that section told a dramatic story "of which the beginning and the ending are very different from each other. Wealth, prosperity, luxury, are . . . the introduction to this story; war, ruin, desolation, the burden; poverty the conclusion." The same words would have described rather accurately practically all of the state and particularly the entire section east of a line drawn from Vermilionville (Lafayette) through Alexandria, to Harrisonburg, and then straight north to the Arkansas border, with the extra fifty-mile-wide strip up the Red River Valley to Grand Ecore and Mansfield. Doctor Sol Smith of Alexandria wrote with the accuracy of firsthand knowledge that the state lay "mangled, rent and palpitating in supreme agony of a ruined and trodden down people."

The dollars-and-cents Civil War loss in Louisiana will never be accurately computed, for many types of financial loss are impossible of even near-accurate estimate, but it is certain that it exceeded that of any other state in the South. The value of all assessable property decreased between 50 per cent and 65 per cent during the four years of war. In 1865, the state banks had a total capital of less than one-third that of 1860; farm land under cultivation was approximately one-half that of 1860 and its prewar value had dropped 65 per cent; farm and plantation livestock holdings had declined approximately the same percentage, and practically all agricultural machinery had been worn out, confiscated, or destroyed. The total livestock-machinery loss, for example, was estimated at about $70,000,000. The capital invested in slave property was a complete loss; after the war A. P. Dostie, an Auditor of Public Accounts under the Radical Governor Michael Hahn, wrote that "$170,000,000 of property has been stricken from among the objects of taxation and raised to the condition of citizens."

Several of Louisiana's ante bellum towns had completely disappeared, among them Dallas, on the Tensas River, and Richmond, in present-day Richland Parish. Practically all of the merchants, sugar and cotton-factory owners, and commission-house proprietors had been completely wiped out, for everything they possessed had been destroyed or confiscated.

Nearly 25 per cent of the men who had gone to war were dead. Many veterans had returned with the "Yankee Mark" upon them —the embedded bullet or piece of shell, or amputated arm or leg, or missing eye, or wound which would not heal. One soldier pointed out that while the unmarked man had his arms and legs to serve him, the "maimed laborer has no future."

The only really financially solvent people in Louisiana at the beginning of the summer of 1865 were the scalawag citizens of the state who had co-operated with Federals during the war years and the hordes of Northern carpetbag speculators and opportunistic businessmen who came with the invading Federal armies to take economic advantage through political opportunities of a people under complete military control.

Wartime Problems of Farmer and Planter. Louisiana agriculturalists faced numerous and unusual wartime problems. The securing of necessary capital became more difficult as the months passed and as the financial-economic situation of the entire South began to reflect the ebb and flow of the tide of military operations. The problem of labor was insurmountable, for as the Federal armies moved into certain areas, slave labor practically ceased and many slaves followed those armies to freedom. Machinery and other equipment could not be replaced or properly repaired, crops spoiled or deteriorated for lack of proper storage facilities, good seed could not be found, harvesting supplies such as cotton bagging or sugar hogsheads were scarce, and the operation of perhaps a $100,000-a-year plantation business was often left to an inexperienced overseer or to the planter's wife. It is truly remarkable that there were so few serious food shortages in many sections of the state.

With the closing of the port of New Orleans, a sizable percentage of the farmer-planter group stopped raising cotton and sugar cane to produce grains, livestock, and truck vegetables. Its production of foodstuffs increased so much that the Ouachita Valley became known as "the Egypt of Louisiana," while the valleys of the lower Mississippi, Bayou Lafourche, Red River, and Bayou Teche, and the alluvial lands of Concordia, Tensas, Madison, and Carroll parishes should have been similarly named. Except in a few small areas, however, agricultural production declined sharply in these sections after Federal invasions began in 1862. There was prosperity only for those farmers and planters willing to sell their products to Federal army quartermasters or to civilian buyers from occupied New Orleans.

In June, 1862, Governor Moore issued orders to burn all cotton which could not be moved out of Federal reach. Shortly before this, however, Kate Stone had echoed the attitude of Southerners when she wrote in her diary that "though the Yankees have gained the land, the people are determined they shall not have its wealth, and from every plantation rises the smoke of burning cotton. . . . And it has thrown a gloom over the country that nothing but news of a great victory could lighten." During the same summer Sarah A. Dorsey "saw the volumes of smoke ascending on every side, for miles and miles, which marked the spots where the planters were burning their crops of cotton . . . in the face of the gunboats ascending the Mississippi River." But as the war progressed, increasing numbers of farmers and planters began to hide their cotton, corn, and other agricultural products, and if the proper opportunity presented itself, to sell to the enemy or to other Louisianians within enemy lines.

Many planters fled to east Texas with their slaves. In the spring of 1863, British Colonel Arthur J. L. Fremantle saw "hundreds" of planters on the Shreveport-Monroe road "driving their families, their slaves, and furniture, towards Texas—in fact, every thing that they could save from the ruin that had befallen them on the approach of the Federal troops." Later in the same year, a Texas newspaper described the "caravans of refugees": "Negro women, their heads wrapped in gaudy bandanas perched high on wagons loaded with chairs, tables, and bedding; stalwart negro men trudging beside the slow-moving vans; dust-covered, bare-footed pickaninnies . . . beside the wagons or stealing a ride on the 'perch pole.'" The abandoned plantations fell to the profit-minded businessmen who followed the invading armies.

The Exchange of Goods. New Orleans was the South's largest port and the Mississippi River the old Union's greatest single avenue of interstate commerce. In late May, 1861, the U. S. S. *Brooklyn* anchored at the mouth of the Mississippi and the captain sent word to Major J. K. Duncan at Fort Jackson that the blockade of Louisiana and the port of New Orleans had officially begun. While river boats continued to run between New Orleans and ports north of Memphis for some time, by the end of the summer the Mississippi River trade had about stopped. Louisiana now had to depend upon its own resources, imports from Mexico, and what few goods could be smuggled through the blockading fleet to satisfy its ordinary and wartime needs.

The Louisiana-Texas-Mexico trade began soon after the establishment of the blockade, and by the fall of 1861, Navasota, Crockett, San Antonio, Laredo, Eagle Pass, and other Texas towns had become bases of operation for Louisiana state and private business agents. The Red River became the great highway for the distribution of Texas-Mexican goods, although the wagon roads running westward from Mansfield, Natchitoches, Alexandria, Opelousas, and Vermilionville became important trading routes. By the beginning of 1862, twenty wagons a day were arriving at, or departing from, Alexandria. The Texas-Mexican trade continued throughout the war and resulted in the exchange of Louisiana cotton, sugar,

102

tobacco, and other staples for dry goods, tools, implements, medicines, paper, small arms and other military supplies, and a considerable amount of luxury goods.

General Butler greatly favored trade between Confederate Louisiana and "Federally Occupied" Louisiana, and although General Banks regarded it as contrary to sound military practice, Northern politicians, businessmen, and speculators increasingly developed their financial, commercial, manufacturing, and agricultural interests in Louisiana throughout the war. Trade between the lines grew steadily, and many soldiers home on furlough commented on the "great change in the ideas and sentiments of the people" when it came to matters of economics. Robert Patrick, for example, found that Clinton residents "were trading liberally with the Yankees, and hauling cotton to them all the time." A British lady living in Woodville, Mississippi, bought goods from wholesalers or their agents in Baton Rouge or New Orleans and retailed them by wagon over a large trade territory in Louisiana. In the fall of 1863, for example, she sold a wagonload of stove pans, cotton and wool cards, household trifles, carpenter's tools, shoebrushes, ladies' finery, woolen cloth, and other goods at Clinton in a single day, and wrote that "The profits were far beyond my expectations." She continued commercial operations throughout the war.

But the distribution of everyday goods was difficult in the back country and even along the waterways of Confederate Louisiana. The railroads soon went out of business because of Federal occupation or the wearing out of rolling stock. Roads steadily deteriorated as grades, fills, bridges, and ferries across bayous and rivers fell into disrepair. Wagons and carts wore out and were difficult to replace. While there were large surpluses of foodstuffs in some sections of the state even in 1864 and 1865, distribution to areas of need was difficult or impossible.

The speculator made huge profits throughout the war at the expense of his country, his state, and his neighbors. Soldiers not infrequently discovered where profitable transactions could be made and reported the information to folks at home. In March, 1865, for example, one soldier conveyed word to his father-in-law in North Louisiana that the Opelousas country offered high-paying profits in the flour trade; he wrote that "if he can save the flour and I can get a wagon, I can make four or five hundred dollars in gold on one load."

Exchange of civilian consumer goods throughout the state posed numerous problems during the entire war. Few of these problems were solved during Governor Moore's administration, and even the energetic activities of Governor Allen did not result in the adequate distribution of the everyday necessities of life.

Manufacture of Consumer and War Goods. Manufacturing had been of only secondary interest to ante bellum Louisianians, and at the beginning of the Confederacy period they had less than

$10,000,000 invested in brick and tile kilns; tanneries; distilleries; sugar refineries; mills for processing lumber, flour, cotton, and iron; and other manufacturing interests. With secession, new factories for the production of cotton and woolen goods, heavy machinery, shoes, rifles, sword bayonets, cannon, and other wartime and peacetime goods were established, along with slaughterhouses, flour mills and gristmills, cotton spinning and weaving mills, and other plants in various sections of the state. In middle June, 1861, the New Orleans *Daily Picayune* admitted that secession and the coming of the war had more encouraged "our manufactured home resources . . . than years of peace could have developed."

But the unusual stimulations of state national autonomy and the organization of the new Southern nation soon quieted down and the establishment of new manufacturing and industrial plants came to a halt. Comparatively little was accomplished during the last two years of Governor Moore's administration, even though the production of the New Orleans area was lost to the rest of the state.

Governor Allen gave new and tremendous stimulus to industrial production and "in the very face of impossiblity, developed the resources of the State to a surprising extent." A plant was established for the making of carbonate of soda, along with two medicinal alcohol distilleries, a turpentine factory in Sabine Parish, a ropewalk and a card factory at Minden, a weaving mill in Claiborne Parish, several slaughterhouses in southern as well as in northern sections, a factory for making cooking utensils, and another for making castor oil. After having surveyed the poor northern Louisiana iron deposits, he purchased for the state a one-fourth interest in a Texas foundry located about a hundred miles west of Shreveport.

The only sources of many ordinary but indispensable medicines were importation from Mexico or smuggling through enemy lines, and by the beginning of 1864 drugs were not only extremely expensive but in many cases almost impossible to procure. In February, 1864, Governor Allen organized a state laboratory under the direction of Doctor Bartholomew Egan at the Mt. Lebanon Female College at Mt. Lebanon and another under Dr. Edward DeLoney and W. D. Winter at Clinton. These laboratories manufactured castor oil, alcohol, medicinal whiskey, turpentine, several drugs, and some drug substitutes from native roots and herbs. Opium was successfully produced at Mt. Lebanon and it was reported that there were no "fatal results from the use of chloroform produced locally."

Salt licks and brine springs had been known in both northern and southern Louisiana since French and Spanish times, but most of the older operations in northern Louisiana had long been closed because of cheaper salt production elsewhere. With the coming of the war, however, the old licks and springs in Bossier, Bienville, and Winn Parishes again became commercially important. The salt works of King, Weeks, Drake, Price, McHenry, Scholars, Hardin,

Mays, and other smaller operators were soon enlarged. Rock salt of "ice-clear transparency" was discovered on Avery Island in May, 1862, and the works there sacked 1,100 bags a day until destroyed by Federal troops in middle April, 1863. Large salt shipments were sent east of the Mississippi River until it was closed during the summer of 1863; after this time smuggling operations were only partially successful.

But Confederate Louisiana could never manufacture sufficient quantities of the thousand and one items of everyday home use. Substitutes were therefore used, and the word "Confederate" took on a new connotation, as Charles P. Roland phrased it, "in the vocabulary of austerity." Sarah Morgan Dawson wrote that "Confederate dresses were old and outmoded; a Confederate bridle was a rope halter; Confederate silver was tin cups and spoons; Confederate flour was unrefined cornmeal." A "Confederate" carriage was any type of hack or light wagon, with covered board seats, and drawn by a pair of mules.

Women and girls, boys and old men, became expert in the manufacture of substitute "Confederate" items. Hats were made of plaited shucks or of palmetto; homespun clothing was dyed with garden-grown indigo, pokeberries, red-oak and other barks; ink was made of magnolia or dogwood bark, pomegranate rinds, or elderberries and green persimmons; shoe blacking was commonly made of a mixture of soot, molasses, egg whites, and vinegar; coffee substitutes were made of parched potatoes, burned meal, parched rye, or roasted acorns, the best being made from okra seed. Candles were made by twisting old rags into wicks and repeatedly dipping them into melted beeswax. On the night of April 28, 1865, Kate Stone wrote in her diary from "Bonnie Castle," her east Texas refuge home: "Just finished a letter to Sarah Wadley, writing with homemade ink, the best we have had for many a day. We also have homemade blacking, just as shiny as the old bought blacking. Truly we are learning many things." The great majority of other Louisiana Confederate girls and women could have written just as graphicly.

Prices. Prices of necessities rose until it became almost impossible for the poor and even middle-class groups to provide food, shelter, and clothing. Confederate money steadily declined in purchasing power. In 1861 soap rose to $1.00 a bar; coffee, to $1.00 a pound; bacon, pork, and ham, to twenty-five cents a pound; lard, to thirty cents a pound; salt, to $10.00 a sack; flour, to $20.00 a barrel; and corn, to $1.00 a bushel. Bread prices were fixed in October at from five cents to twenty cents for loaves weighing from fourteen ounces to fifty-four ounces. Other food prices were rising to "famine figures."

Prices steadily advanced in 1862, and soldiers began to complain of the "very little clothing and very scanty fare provided for us." A pair of good soldier's boots were reported to cost $40.00 a pair, while ordinary "walking shoes" cost $15.00 and were hard to get. Silk material was selling, when it could be found, for as high as $500.00 a yard, but few ladies wore silk any more. Flour now cost $25.00 a barrel; eggs, $1.00 a dozen; butter, $1.00 a pound; corn, $1.25 a bushel. A loaf of bread could still be purchased in New Orleans for only five cents, but it weighed only seven ounces.

By the fall of 1863 beef had advanced to forty cents a pound; flour, to $3.00 a peck; salt, to $130.00 per sack in areas where transportation was lacking; quinine, to $20.00 an ounce. Shreveport prices in 1864 were possibly above those in some other sections: butter, $5.00 a pound; eggs, $5.00 a dozen; beans, $2.50 a quart; apples, twenty-five to fifty cents each; melons, $1.00 to $5.00 each; bacon and hams, seventy-five cents a pound and up. During the last year of the war prices went even higher, soared to "figures never heard of before" in areas of real scarcity, and became truly astronomical in a few sections. One man wrote that before the war he went to market with the money in his pocket and brought back his purchases in a basket; "now, I take the money in the basket, and bring the things home in my pocket."

Looting and Wholesale Destruction. In April, 1863, General U. S. Grant wrote that the "Rebellion has assumed that shape now that it can only terminate by the complete subjugation of the South or the overthrow of the Government. It is our duty, therefore, to use every means to weaken the enemy, by destroying their means of subsistence, withdrawing their means of cultivating their fields, and in every other way possible." The Northern general need not have written the communique insofar as Louisiana was concerned, for the pillage and destruction of property in that state had begun during the preceding summer. Historians who have called the Civil War the "last gentlemen's war" have apparently done little, if any, real research on what actually occurred in the Red River Valley and in the Louisiana plantation sections to the west of Vicksburg; despite the publicity given Sherman's march through Georgia, the dollar value of the property loss there did not compare with the loss in the Bayou State. And the proposition can be seriously debated that such looting and destruction of private property in country and town had little, if any, influence on the final outcome of the war.

There is a broad distinction between "looting and pillage" and "living off the country." Armies of both North and South generally lived, to a greater or lesser degree, off the country through which they marched, and it is safe to say that the areas through which either army passed were generally picked clean of edible animals, fowls, grains, vegetables, and fruits. But there was a great deal of needless and deliberate Federal destruction of property in Louisiana. Northern soldier James K. Hosmer admitted that "We were turned loose . . . to kill cattle, pigs, and poultry. All this marauding went on ruthlessly and wastefully. We left the road behind us foul with the odor of decaying carcasses."

Only one Federal commander, Admiral David G. Farragut, "ordered" the destruction of Louisiana towns. Donaldsonville was shelled and burned in August, 1862, and left "a heap of ruins" for "nearly every house has been destroyed"; after heavy bombardment the following year, Bayou Sara was described as "a blackened skeleton of chimneys arising from rubble heaps." But fires "broke out" in more than one Federal-army-occupied town. "The handsome State-House—a pile of well-designed Norman architecture, once the pride of the little city" of Baton Rouge—burned on the night of December 28, 1862. Berwick City burned in 1863. The following year General A. J. Smith's men fired Alexandria as the Federal troops evacuated the town.

Years after the war, Federal General James Tuttle, in a speech at Des Moines, Iowa, humorously boasted that he was the "General Tuttle whose troops, on the march from Milliken's Bend to Grand Gulf, burned so many fine houses on Lake St. Joseph, among them the finest residence in all the southern country, that of Col. Bowie. . . . The Bowie mansion . . . was the grandest house I ever saw or read about." Practically all of the many Federal soldiers who wrote of their Louisiana army experiences mentioned the looting of farm, plantation, and village homes along the routes of march.

Extant plantation diaries also record the wanton destruction and pillage. At one plantation, "our carriages and wagons" were loaded and driven away "full of our silver and china and the best of our furniture"; at another the Federals "took up everything that could be used and destroyed what could not be used"; at another "they dragged out the beautiful rose-wood furniture and made bonfires of it, while they played Yankee Doodle and Hail Columbia on grand Pleyel and Erard pianos, and danced round the fires fed by such costly fuel."

While it may have been difficult to have prevented pillaging by large bodies of soldiers in the field or in line of march, it should not have been impossible for commanding officers to have enforced their orders in occupied towns. The sack of towns, then, was accomplished only through the approval, the negligence, or the inefficiency of commanding officers; in any case, they must accept the responsibility and the blame. Many Federals simply acted the role of Pontius Pilate, as did James Croushore: "Yesterday my colored servant George brought in ten pounds or so of solid old table silver. I had no means of restoring it to the owner . . . so I simplified the situation by telling George to clear out with it and never let me see it again."

Some officers defended the actions of pillagers: "The owners of all this are rebels, who have fled our approach, not waiting to take the oath of allegiance. It is right, therefore to confiscate their property." But some Federal officers protested wanton and unnecessary destruction and stealing. Gunboat Captain Clinton B. Fisk, while on duty in northeastern Louisiana in 1862, wrote to an army division commander: "GENERAL: I am pained to witness the pillaging, plundering, and irregular foraging on the part of some of the commands of this expedition. . . . I hand you herewith an order I have just issued, and, with the grace of God sustaining me, I will enforce it if I have to shoot men both in and out of shoulder-straps. We cannot make good soldiers of thieves and robbers, neither can we expect success to follow us if we thus outrage every principle of truth and justice. I am ashamed when I see our good cause thus prejudiced."

General Thomas Williams, shortly before his death at the Battle of Baton Rouge, reported: "I regret to say I believe there is just ground against the Wisconsin and Michigan regiments for the charge of pillaging and marauding preferred against them by the inhabitants of Kenner Station. . . . These regiments, officers and men, with rare exceptions, appear to be wholly destitute of the moral sense. . . ."

Lieutenant F. A. Roe of the United States Navy protested from Donaldsonville to Commodore Henry W. Morris, on September 11, 1862:

I respectfully request instructions if the guns of the *Kathahdin* are to be used for the protection of soldiers upon a marauding expedition, and if I am to use them in the protection of drunken, undisciplined, and licentious troops in the wanton pillaging of a private mansion. . . . I am desirous of encountering enemies and of injuring them in every manly manner, but I cannot further prostitute the dignity of my profession, as I conceive I have done today. . . . It is disgraceful and humiliating to me to be ordered on guard duty of soldiers employed in pillaging ladies' dresses and petticoats, and I respectfully request that I may be relieved from such service.

Commodore Morris simply bucked the communication up to General Benjamin F. Butler at New Orleans. Butler did nothing but endorse the document on the back as the "improper, bombastic, and ridiculous rhodomontade of a sub-lieutenant of the Navy."

XIII

Life of the People During Wartime

The Folks at Home. Louisiana's average Johnny Reb left his
plow, fishing boat, timber axe, or whatever the tools of his trade
were, and went off to war, leaving his wife and children to raise
what crops or vegetables they could and to otherwise shift for
themselves, with perhaps some assistance from the home parish or
town. His officers generally left slaves, large farms or plantations,
or businesses. An officer's family had little fear of actual want,
unless the destroying enemy came near, but Johnny's wife and children, at least during the last year of the war, frequently went
hungry. Both families suffered many hardships to which they were
unaccustomed and supported Louisiana's war effort as best they
could.

It has been said that the women of the South were more loyal to
the Confederacy than were the men; certainly the women of Louisiana worked with strong loyalty and steady *esprit de corps.* Singly,
in small groups, and in larger organizations, they sewed and
knitted and darned, made uniforms and straw, palmetto, or cloth
hats, tanned leather, collected materials for "hospital boxes," made
blankets and gloves and numerous little unimportant things that
made Johnny Reb's life in the field bearable. They managed plantations, operated businesses, kept the home, concocted remedies and
medicines, worked in the fields or at trades in villages and towns,
raised animals and fowls and gardened, and then canned, holed-in,
dried, cribbed, smoked, salted, pickled, fried-down, jerked, and
otherwise preserved meats and fruits and vegetables against coming days of scarcity.

Long after the war, Grace King wrote: "Mamma and Grand-
mamma took off their fine bonnets, and after rolling their wide
strings, laid them away on the top shelf of an armoire. Four years
later they took them out and put them on again." Her words well
illustrate the life metamorphosis of Southern women from peace to
war to peace. During the conflict, Kate Stone wrote that "in proportion as we have been a race of haughty, indolent, and waited-on
people, so now are we ready to do away with all forms and work

and wait on ourselves." But hunger and privation became commonplace in the Confederacy, and Mrs. Edward Beaumont's children "often asked why we had no holidays now—no Fourth of July, no Christmas and Santa Claus? And when I spoke to them of the many children at this time reduced to hunger and rags by the ravages of war, they grew silent, wondering, but not understanding how all this could be."

Cachez les apparences—hide appearances; keep quiet about the family troubles—became watchwords of not only the Creoles, but of all Louisiana women left at home. Throughout the war, they wore their patriotism and their loyalties as chips on their shoulders, and dared Yankees to knock them off. After Lawrence Van Alstyne had entered a South Louisiana yard to get some oranges and had been discovered by a young girl, who gave him some of the fruit and then ordered him out, he wrote: "I never saw so much scorn on a face before. Why I stood there like a chicken thief caught in the act, and then carried off the oranges, I don't now know. If the Rebels were all like her I would resign and go home at once, for she did actually scare my wits all away from me." Another Yankee soldier once remarked: "I wonder if these Southern girls can love as they hate? If they can, it would be well worth one's trying to get one of them."

There were many Louisiana war heroines, most of whom were unheralded and unsung. Grace King's mother smuggled money through the lines by sewing it up with the sawdust-and-rag stuffing of her daughter's ugly doll. Unidentified was the northeast Louisiana teen-age girl who guided a detachment of Captain Eli Bowman's force, on its way to attack Waterproof, through the night to the Black River ford and the road beyond. Mrs. William Kirby, after regularly running the blockade out of Baton Rouge, was finally arrested, "convicted as a spy and sentenced to serve during the continuance of the war in close confinement on Ship Island." Mrs. Fannie Beers served as an army nurse throughout the war. After the Battle of New Carthage two women rowed through the Federal lines in a small boat, picked up the body of a young Confederate lying on the levee, rowed back through the lines, and then, Antigone-like, dug a grave and performed funeral rites over his body. Two months later they were seen, with two small children, "camped by the roadside in Franklin Parish, with a few boards over their heads, as a temporary shelter from the rain and sun." A few wives of officers and ordinary Johnny Rebs accompanied their husbands on field campaigns, and cooked, washed, mended clothing, and nursed the sick and wounded.

While old men generally stayed at home and "took over" for sons and grandsons, "old war horses" in their sixties and even seventies were not unknown. Most of the "old stay-at-homes" joined the Home Guards and went on regular night patrols in areas of unrest or where guerrillas or jayhawkers operated. They all performed physical labor beyond their strength; many died before their time and were buried in Confederate Gray.

The record of the Louisiana "Confederate" Free Negro and the "loyal" slave during the years of war has never been adequately recounted. Most of the Free Negroes sided with the South, and while they could not officially join the army, many served in civilian capacities. Much has been made of the loyalty of Southern slaves, but strong loyalties were generally confined to house servants or to slaves who were owned by small planters or farmers and who lived in close relationship to the owner and his family. A good many field hands "took off," "refugeed" at New Orleans or other occupied towns, or enlisted in the Federal army.

The great majority of slaves, however, continued their ordinary slave lives with little change in routine until the coming of Federal military forces. They were protected as much as possible, and General Richard Taylor later wrote: "It was a curious feature of the war that the Southern people would cheerfully send their sons to battle, but kept their slaves out of danger." The statements of some historians that Southerners lived in constant fear of slave insurrections during the war years is simply not borne out by the facts. British news correspondent William H. Russell wrote from Louisiana that "none of the Southern gentlemen have the smallest apprehension of a servile insurrection," and Charles Dudley Warner stated that Southerners never forgot "the security with which the white families dwelt in the midst of a black population while all the white men were absent in the field."

Cornbread and Substitute Coffee. Louisianians were forced to change their dietary habits during the first six months of the war because of the Federal blockade and the rapid increase in prices. Spices, wines and liquors, preserved fruits, and other such domestic or imported goods soon disappeared from their tables. Despite the tremendous increase in acreage planted to food crops in 1861 and thereafter, food shortages in some sections of the state became critical during the last two years of the war. Sarah Dorsey wrote that after January, 1864, Governor Allen spent much time with the problem of civilian food supply and that he received many "letters from ladies belonging to the most distinguished families in our unhappy State, begging for a few pounds of meal, flour, sugar, and molasses." While Allen kept wagon trains running back and forth into east Texas, the problems of food supply and distribution were never solved. Although salt production increased during each year of the war, the supply never satisfied the demand. In some sections the lack of salt prevented the preservation of meat, and more than one soldier, as did Robert Patrick, "boiled down brine to make salt to send to mother." Plantation or farm families often dug up the dirt in smokehouses, where meat had been smoked and salted for many years, soaked it in large kettles, and then boiled the water, thus securing small amounts of salt.

111

The blockade soon cut the supply of coffee, although small amounts were smuggled through the lines or imported from Mexico. What little coffee the family hoarded was mixed with practically anything of a brownish, parched nature which would stretch the real article. Tea was just as difficult to secure, so many substitutes were used, sassafras tea being generally the most popular.

The farm production of home-cured meats greatly increased, and even planters and townfolk learned the art of butchering and meat cutting and the processes of salting and smoking. Lard, sausage, and salt meat were sometimes packaged in small amounts and hidden against the day when Federal troopers rode into the yard. But the time came when cracked corn, parched and eaten dry or soaked in hot water, was for many the only food to be had. As early as May, 1862, Kate Stone wrote: "It seems odd to be expecting company and no flour or any 'boughten' delicacy to regale them on, but we have been on a strict 'war footing' for some time."

A few who were profiting from the war, however, ate well throughout the months when others were practically starving. Late in 1864, one Alexandria citizen wrote that he had recently dined at a friend's home where "The table groaned with a profusion of good things, and I am ashamed to say I ate until I made myself sick." In late March, 1865, the same individual wrote that "I think I am very bad off, and yet I have never ceased using coffee, have an abundance of excellent bacon and corn beef and never sit down to my table without good biscuits and better eggbread."

Homespun Dresses and Dyed Linsey Pants. Early in 1862, Kate Stone wrote: ". . . no frills and furbelows for us. Affairs are too grave to think of dress." Later that same year, she commented that "Fashion is an obsolete word and just to be decently clad is all we expect." Broadcloth and silk and "hoop skirts of crinoline" may have been indispensable when ante bellum fashion ruled the land of Louisiana, but during the war women wore dresses and coats of rough, often hand-woven material, and no one "looked odd." However, the Southern woman frequently stole furtive glances at the fashion drawings in back numbers or smuggled issues of Yankee-printed *Harper's New Monthly Magazine* or *Godey's Lady's Book,* for her love of new fashions and pretty clothes, as one lady said, was merely "scotched . . . not killed."

Men generally discarded broadcloth and other such materials and used home-dyed linsey or wool. Vests went out of fashion and were replaced by "overshirts" which took the place of overcoats. Shoes were repaired until there was nothing left to "repair to." They were even made with cloth tops and pigskin soles, and only occasionally of "good leather." Prewar hats were only worn on special occasions; gentlemen wore headpieces made of palmetto, or rye, wheat or oat straw, or plaited from odd bits of cloth.

The spinning wheel and the loom were brought back into use, just like "going back to the days of the Revolution," and unaccustomed fingers were soon busy with the ancient household arts of spinning and dying and weaving. Old wood or bone buttons were covered or re-covered with cloth of great age; hats which mother had worn or in which grandmother had promenaded on the steamboat going down to New Orleans were restitched and retrimmed for girls to wear when their soldiers came home on leave; ornaments from long ago were sewn to dresses which would now be worn to sewing parties, to church, and to the funerals of Southern heroes who had died for the Confederacy.

Social Life. Social life in village, town, and country declined as the hardships and privations of war increased over the entire state. Professional entertainment ceased altogether outside occupied New Orleans, for the male members of stage companies, concert-artist groups, bands, circuses, and other entertainment media had gone to war. Homemade entertainment on an unadorned, austere scale became the almost unbroken rule. In towns and villages there were "party dances," picnics, church or religious meetings, speechmaking, home-talent concerts by glee clubs and individual artists, and military or civilian philanthropic gatherings of various types for the purpose of raising money. In smaller villages and in the country, families and neighbors enjoyed card or other games at home, fishing and hunting expeditions, home dances, fish fries, barbecues, and other small-group sports and amusements.

Unquestionably the favorite social activity was the entertaining of soldiers on furlough or those who had been invalided home for a short period. Grace King recalled being "carried up the high levee where Papa stood waiting for us. After that the good supper, big fires, and soft, warm beds, where sleep came for the children to the pleasant tune of talk over what was past." Kate Stone described the activities of the family when one of her brothers arrived home on sick leave: "He looks taller and has lost forty pounds. Home life and love will soon build him up. He came at dusk. We have kept him talking until eleven, and that was not wise, as of course he is tired. . . . Our heartfelt thanks go up to God for having returned to us our best beloved brother."

Colonel Winchester Hall was "invalided" on "special exchange" for a short period in occupied New Orleans. Late one afternoon, as he approached a sidewalk, ". . . four little girls, prettily dressed, stopped in their walk and awaited me. One of them approached me and offered her hand, saying 'We are Confederates.' I shook hands with three of them, but the other—of some six summers—stood shyly apart; the little spokeswoman then pointed, as though she wanted me to go to the fourth one, and said, 'She is a rebel too.' So I went up and shook hands with the little rebel."

Home-talent concerts were sure-fire money raisers, for the entire community bought high-priced tickets and crowded into the hall. On October 5, 1864, for example, the "grand vocal and instrumental concert" of the Shreveport Glee Club, given at the request of Governor Allen, netted "the handsome amount of $5,000." In smaller towns, home talent frequently left something to be desired; let Robert Patrick describe, in his own inimitable fashion, some of the principals at a Clinton concert in December, 1862;

Miss Jane Stoke devoted herself entirely to the piano. . . . How graceful she looked while sitting at the piano, her beautiful neck about as long as my arm and as large as a broom-stick . . . her beautiful rounded, snow-white arms . . . look like the leg bones of a turkey after all the flesh has been taken off, or a well-rope with a knot tied in it. . . . Taking her altogether, she looked like the devil as she was led to the piano and her back seemed as though it would break in two, she was so long and limber. . . .

Mrs. Comstock next attracted my attention. She looked as ugly as ever. She sang in opera style and piled on some of the most excruciating agonies. . . .

Mrs. Ball thought she sang very well and evidently appreciated her own music if no one else did. Her mouth shut and opened like a rat-trap.

Singing was a popular diversion and copies of popular songs, along with *Hopkins' New Orleans 5¢ Song Book* and the *Southern Flag Song Book*, passed from hand to hand while the music and words were copied. New Orleans had several music houses, including those of A. E. Blackmar, Philip Werlein, L. Grunewald, A. G. Gardner, and Charles Horst, which published sentimental songs, as well as those designed to stir the blood of the patriotic Southerner. Blackmar published "The Bonnie Blue Flag" and Werlein brought out "Dixie," for which act Butler later condemned him to a few weeks in jail as the publisher of a "seditious" work. Favorite patriotic songs included "The Southern Marseillaise," "The Wearing of the Grey," "God and Our Rights," and "For Bales," a song lampooning Banks's Red River Expedition of 1864 which soon became famous as "When Johnny Comes Marching Home."

Education. The sixteen-year period beginning in the spring of 1861 forms the most harrowing chapter in the entire history of Louisiana education. The war years brought an almost complete cessation of elementary, secondary, and higher educational activities, and little was accomplished during the years of military occupation from 1865 to the spring of 1877.

Public education was just becoming acceptable and was beginning to make real progress when the war began. Henry Avery had become state superintendent, available educational funds had increased to more than $600,000, Baton Rouge had a high school ready to begin functioning in a $20,000 house donated by the police jury, the public schools were reaching nearly 50 per cent of the children of school age, and parochial schools were improving instruction.

While there was comparatively little change in the work of the public schools in 1861, except that most of the Northern teachers went home, problems had greatly increased by the beginning of the following school year. The Legislature appropriated nearly $500,000 to public education, but little of this sum was used for that purpose; most of the male teachers and many of the older male students had marched off to war. By 1863 there was no money, and public schools and private academies were in a completely demoralized condition. The few Southern textbooks which had been printed were difficult to secure, and Johnson's and Davies' arithmetics, McGuffey's readers, and Webster's spellers were still in general use. The first free school textbook in Louisiana, the *Louisiana English Grammar*, was published by order of Governor Allen and printed at the office of the *South-Western* at Shreveport in 1865, but few copies were actually distributed.

When General Butler reopened the New Orleans schools in 1862 on a completely integrated white-Negro basis, with Northern teachers generally in charge, few white students attended. Special schools were organized by Federal military commanders in other occupied areas for the children of the newly freed Negroes. Most Northern teachers, however, who followed the Federal armies into Louisiana never became really interested in Negro education because the students were incorrigible and because they generally excelled, as one teacher phrased it, only in "subjects which involved a maximum of memory and a minimum of reasoning."

The net result of the breakdown of elementary and secondary education during the war years was that many children of school age who did not have instruction at home never learned to read, or postponed their education until after the war or even until after the restoration of white supremacy in 1877.

Collegiate education practically ceased throughout the state. The newly opened State Seminary of Learning and Military Academy suspended operations in June, 1861. All of the students, except one who enlisted in the Federal navy, joined the Confederate service. The institution led a checkered existence until General Banks occupied the area in 1863, and was sacked in 1864 by the troops of General T. Kilby Smith, who fortunately, however, was able to save many of the institution's records. Modern military historian John D. Winters has written: "The Seminary probably contributed more young men, instructors, and equipment to the Confederacy than any other college. Cadets were sought as drillmasters in camps from Louisiana to Virginia."

Literature and the Press in Wartime. The rural civilization of the ante bellum South had been a literature-consuming rather than a literature-producing culture, and most of the comparatively few Southern writers laid down their pens in 1861, not to take them up again until the end of the war. Charles Gayarré, the state's best-known historian and author, spent the war years at "Roncal," his country home near Amite, and produced practically nothing. A few authors too old for military service continued their work but did

115

not attempt to publish until after the war ended; poet John Augustin, for example, published his *War Flowers* in 1865. While the writing of soldier and civilian letters and the keeping of diaries and journals increased to a fantastic degree as the months of the war passed, little of this material was literary in quality, although it vividly portrayed soldier and civilian life.

Because of the blockade and because they lacked funds to buy books, as Basil Gildersleeve has indicated, the current United States and world literature of those years "was a blank to most Confederates. Few books got across the line." While large consignments of bibles, new testaments, and bible tracts were smuggled in, comparatively little else came from abroad. A few works, however, were reprinted in the South; Victor Hugo's *Les Miserables* was immensely popular with soldiers, who called it "Lee's Miserables," and the works of Louise Muhlbach, known as "Lou Mealbag," were passed from friend to friend or became mediums of exchange in floating crap games or card games.

But if the Confederate could not get currently published books, he could read and reread those already in Southern stores or in private libraries. Being conservative and not particularly liking American literature anyway, he went back to his English, European, and ancient classics. Older men reviewed their Latin and Greek; younger men read history, poetry, essays, novels, travel accounts, and dramas. While many sighed, as did J. D. B. DeBow "to know what was doing in the great outside literary world," most of them were content, for the time being at least, to read the classics and the "old standard" books.

Newspapers rapidly went out of business, because many of their editors, owners, reporters, and printers went off to war, not infrequently leaving a short but eloquent sign to that effect scrawled on the front door, or because newsprint and ink soon became impossible of procurement. Only the larger towns were able to support poorly printed sheets. In New Orleans, editors soon ran afoul of Butler, and their newspapers were closed up or placed under such strict censorship that they were of no interest to Southerners. The *Bee, Commerical Bulletin, Crescent, Daily Advocate, Picayune,* and others were suppressed and the *Delta* was placed in Federal hands. By the end of 1861 some parishes had no newspapers at all and more than one parish clerk and police-jury secretary had to post official notices on the front door of the courthouse because legal publication was impossible. A good many weaker and small-town newspapers were never able to resume publication after the war.

Religion. Numerous ministers, priests, and rabbis marched off to war with the members of their congregations, most of them to serve in various army religious capacities but some as soldiers in the ranks; one of them became a general. Many clergymen had preached that secession and the establishment of a Southern Confederacy was necessary "to protect religion against the inroads of

116

rationalism and infidelity"; now they supported the war as a holy cause.

While slave religious activity declined during the war, owing to the lack of plantation support, the fires of white faith burned with greater intensity. Church members were short of money but contributed as generously as possible to the support of regular ministers and lay preachers. Revivals and camp meetings increased in number, both in the army and in areas far removed from military campaigns.

Many officers and enlisted men became regular in their attendance at religious meetings and eventually were baptized. Federal soldiers not infrequently attended services in towns through which they passed; on July 26, 1863, Lawrence Van Alstyne wrote: "Went to church to-day. It was a Catholic church and the sermon was in Latin, so I don't know whether he prayed for or against us. . . . I was ashamed of my clothes, but they were my best, and none of them could say more than that." One of the most graphic descriptions of a Louisiana army "preaching" was written by Texan Joseph P. Blessington:

A huge shelter protected the assembly from the night-dews. Rough seats, made of logs, covered the space beneath this shelter. Stands, on which were built fires from pine knots, shed a lurid light over the vast concourse. The hymns sung would rise in rich cadences, floating away on the evening breeze in solemn, harmonious strains, followed by an earnest prayer and an impassioned and eloquent discourse. It was a strange spectacle to witness these rough, bronzed soldiers, inured to danger and hardships, making bloodshed the chief aim of their lives, exposed to the evil influences of a soldier's dissipated and reckless existence, thus striving to seek a "home not made with hands, eternal in the heavens."

117

Aftermath and Legend

Johnny Reb of Louisiana straggled homeward during that chilly spring of 1865, an incredibly thin, spraddle-legged fellow with a carcass remindful of a tough old hickory barrel deeply impregnated with salts and bitter flavors and topped by a face like a blunted axe blade, the whole wrapped in a hopelessly-dirty, battered old hat, hand-sewn, patched, faded, tattered pants and coat, both shrunken to short proportions, a dingy, threadbare, colorless shirt, and ill-fitting, travel-worn old shoes. The Southern world at that time was made up of poorly and oddly dressed people, but the returning Confederate soldier led the company.

With the exception of bustling New Orleans—where the occupying Federal army and civil authorities were headquartered and where ships and steamboats were busy carrying supplies and soldiers, where hotels and rooming houses were filled, where theaters and bars and gambling houses entertained businessmen and Northern speculators and carpetbaggers of all degrees—the land of Louisiana was run-down and bedraggled, pockmarked by war, inhabited by hungry, grief-burdened, stiff-lipped men and women. Throughout the state there were abandoned, burnt-out, silent areas where one could almost hear the sound of his own footsteps and the sound of his own breathing, where the snapping of a twig was as sharp and startling as the crack of a rifle. The rider of the horse that was red had been there, and the rider of the pale horse, too, and Hell had followed behind them. America has known no tragedies like those which filled the land of the South at the beginning of that summer of 1865.

So the tired and worn-out veterans came home. They were all old men, old before their time. They had missed the glorious, nocturne, irreplaceable days of youth. They had marched off to war with a boy's smell on them, had jumped straight from boyhood to manhood, and many had run through the full strength of their manhood years in a few short months. Now when the last flag and the last guidon had fallen, they straightened, dressed their lines, to face without flinching the twelve tragic years of Federal shame which were to come. Their high-strung pride was still there, a thing that

118

would indelibly mark them for the rest of their days. The old courage was still written on their faces, particularly in their eyes, the courage which recalled endless marches of endless miles along endless roads, a hundred rivers crossed, a thousand burned-out campfires, and scores of headlong charges, bloody melees, swift pursuits, or retreats filled with despair and death. But there was also something not seen but rather strongly felt, something that told a person that when future troubles came these men would still stand.

And stand they did, against a North that believed that the South had committed crimes against nature, the Constitution, the old Union, and the memory of Washington and Jefferson. If there was to be no punishment, then there had been no crime. But the South was a criminal and therefore should be punished. So the years of the so-called "Reconstruction" of the South followed the collapse of the Confederacy in 1865, twelve years of Federal military occupation and governmental control during which the South's ways of life were demolished and its social order was reversed, and during which little was done by an avenging government to heal the bleeding wounds of a desperately wounded land. The South finally reconstructed itself, but it took a long time, beyond even the turn of the twentieth century. Memories of the war would last a long time in Louisiana and in the other states, but while the South accepted the humiliation of military defeat in its struggle for independence, it never accepted the abuses of the years of postwar military occupation.

Southerners never felt any guilt from the war and they therefore never felt that it was incumbent upon them to atone for a guilt which they never admitted. If it took regret to earn forgiveness, then they were never forgiven, for they never regretted the days and years of the Southern Confederacy. They still accepted the words of Bishop Leonidas Polk to the venerable Bishop William Meade in 1861: "We of the Confederate States are the last bulwarks of civil . . . liberty; we fight for our hearthstones. . . . When I accept a commission in the Confederate army, therefore, I not only perform the duties of a good citizen, but contend for the principles which lie at the foundation of our social, political, and religious polity."

The people of the North forgot that from 1861 to 1865 Southerners had been "Confederates" and not "Americans," for the Confederate States of America had been their country and they had fought to win the independence of that country just as their ancestors had fought to win the independence of the old Union. Southerners did not become "Americans" again until time healed the old wounds. Could anyone have expected otherwise? Could the memory of four years of patriotism and loyalty and fighting in defense of a country be erased in one year, or in one decade, or even in the rest of a Confederate lifetime? The answer was perhaps best given by Judge Henry L. Duffel of Donaldsonville in 1882, when he said: "Is it not enough that one has carried triumphantly over a hundred bloody fields the beloved Confederate flag, and furled it only when the immortal Lee himself had surrendered his sword?"

So the Johnny Rebs of Louisiana and of the South slowly became Americans again and grew old and became grandfathers and great-uncles, and their wives became grandmothers and great-aunts who also aged, but with grace and gentleness, and who seldom talked about the past or the hardships of the war or its aftermath. They all had a dignified manner and if they wore it somewhat ceremoniously on occasion as one would wear clothing they should be forgiven, for they remembered the days when formality and politeness had been a fundamental part of life itself.

The grandfathers and great-uncles became heroes to wide-eyed and large-eared children who watched and listened—and the hero worship of a child is a strange and wonderful thing. Through these veterans the youth of Louisiana relived the days of Southern glory. Robert E. Lee and Alfred Mouton, Leonidas Polk and Dick Taylor, and a thousand other Confederates were men of real flesh and blood. Shiloh, Gettysburg, Mansfield, Pleasant Hill, Chickamauga, Baton Rouge, Port Hudson, Grand Coteau, and numerous other names meant bloody battles which had been lost or won under the banner of the Southern Cross. Appomattox was a hallowed place where the gallant Lee had surrendered his poorly armed and hungry little band of heroes rather than have them cut to pieces as had Leonidas his men at Thermopylae. They filled some of their stories so full of imagination and embellishment that they could not be believed; others were so simple and unadorned that their stark, matter-of-fact plainness made them obviously real and true. And if a narrator became emotionally excited, he was forgiven, for his story brought back the comrades of that valiant time or the memory of some half-forgotten incident now magnified and made warm and happy by the passage of the years, and it wiped out Appomattox, restored the Southern Confederacy to its young manhood days of strength, unfurled again the emblem of the Stars and Bars.

The old soldiers still wore their suits of Confederate Gray, with the little buttons of the "Southern Cross of the Confederacy" on their lapels. And in time all of them became officers, for there were generals, hosts of colonels, numerous majors, and lesser numbers of captains and lieutenants. One British traveler in Louisiana wrote with rare understanding that "everybody is either a general, colonel, or major; and the best rule perhaps, if you don't know exactly what a man is, is to call him General. If he is a general, you are right; and if he isn't, he will excuse the mistake."

For as long as they lived, the old soldiers would sit around the town hall or depot or steamboat landing or parish courthouse, soaking up the afternoon sun and reliving the days of the war. Sometimes their faces would be high-lighted with humor; on other occasions their lips would be folded into tight lines perhaps indicating that they were off to war again and were thinking of battles or of comrades who had fallen in the fore ranks of attacking waves or defending lines. At times there would be long silences, and you did not ask questions, not if you respected their memories, for an old soldier is entitled to uninterrupted time to think of what is private to himself alone. After some of these silences two old seat-mates might gaze at each other for a moment, sharing a short eternity of comradeship, thinking possibly that the only thing really worse than dying young was in living too long, for their romantic, heroic world had long since passed into history.

So the generation which had fought the War for Southern Independence departed from the scenes of living men. But their memories of a nation which did not live to full maturity did not die with them, for to all Southerners time became the tangible dimension of all things and the past became an indispensable part of the present. Southerners looked backward to a yesterday that had been gloriously lived and back beyond the war to the days of an Old South which would never be forgotten; and their recollections and memories were woven into the tight and lasting fabric of a living legend which in these modern days of changing moral, social, cultural, economic, and governmental values should always be remembered as a treasured portion of the Southern Heritage.

Index

124